Elaine's World

Elaine C. Smith

ELAINE'S WORLD

FIRST PUBLISHED 1998
BY B&W PUBLISHING LTD
EDINBURGH

ISBN 1 873631 91 X

COVER PHOTOGRAPH
COURTESY OF THE LOOK AGENCY.

PICTURE CREDITS: ALL PHOTOS © ELAINE C. SMITH
EXCEPT RAB C. NESBITT PHOTOS © BBC SCOTLAND
AND 'CATERPILLAR' & NIPPY SWEETIES © ALAN WYLIE

DESIGN: WINFORTUNE & ASSOCIATES

PRINTED BY WSOY

CONTENTS

FOR
KATIE & HANNAH,
BOB & ALL MY FAMILY

INTRODUCTION

Really this book should be called "Well, how the hell did I end up here?" It was never my intention to be an actor, it was not even in the realms of the possible for me. Never, ever, mentioned in the career talks that my parents had with me. They never said "Don't worry, if you don't get into teacher training college, why don't you write to a few agents and see if you can get some acting jobs." Eh? Not a chance. The approved list of careers included doctors, lawyers and teachers—at a push, maybe, a job in a bank. Actor, entertainer, singer was not even a purposeful omission, it just did not exist. The way my life started out

I don't think that ending up an actor or self-confessed rabble rouser was really on the cards.

When you were brought up in working-class Lanarkshire in the 1960s and 70s you got to know your lot in life very quickly. Those who broke the rules with regard to what their role was supposed to be were dealt with harshly—unless you became a success and then everyone would claim to know you or your wee sister or your second cousin who played accordion in an Orange band in New Stevenson in 1967! At this point in my life I realise that I must have had a Primary 3 class of 400 judging by the number of people claiming to have been at school with me.

Anyway, as with all good tales, the Greeks have a great expression for those who don't fully comply with their lot. They would say that I have overstepped my "Moira" i.e. my allotted role in life. But now that I have had a chance to reflect, I can't help thinking that maybe I haven't. Maybe the role that was allotted to me by my surroundings and upbringing was not the one that I was meant to play. At the ripe old age of 40, I think I have finally come to terms with the fact that being a performer and a very public person really is my allotted role in life, and not to have followed this path would have been wrong.

Perhaps that is why it has taken me so long to deal with my life and feel comfortable with it. To say that I have always felt at home in this public performance of a life would be very wrong. I may appear to be at home with it, but there have been many years of feeling wrong, insecure, worthless, not talented or good enough and generally that this is not what I should be doing.

What I should be doing is behaving. What I should be doing is being a good girl.

I should be a good girl and not open my mouth about things that the men are supposed to talk about, like comedy or football or politics. I should support men and not want to be top of the bill, I should be happy that men are looking after everything and that women are ignored or patronised or pigeonholed into that "Oh yes, she's that lippy, busty, Glasgow woman who's involved in comedy—funny but very cosy and working-class. Couldn't ever be a player, so let's dismiss her immediately. What do you mean she won't go away? She's refusing. How can she do that! Christ she can't be that confident, she didn't go to public school! What? She's got a degree, shit. I blame the sixties for allowing these types to get on in education and see how the rest of us live. Makes them too difficult to dismiss . . . bloody women."

Sorry, I got a bit too bitter and twisted there, a failing I know. Add it to the list.

However there is a truth in there for most of the women I have met in my life who are trying to do anything outwith their "Moiras".

I know that I should be a good girl. Life would be so much easier. I should stick in at school, do well, but not too well or the boys won't fancy me. I should get my Highers and get to teacher training college (Primary, of course, Secondary means that you have got a degree and that is too scary for the peer group and your neighbours to deal with and it cuts out all the guys who work in the steelworks who fancy you until they find out that you're brainy).

No, be a good girl. Don't sleep around because then you can't have a big white wedding and men don't want "soiled goods". Stay a virgin, act innocent, be compliant, lie—but be a good girl.

Don't be the funny one that tells better gags than the guys. Don't get in first with an answer or a punchline, be funny as one of a gang but not as a girlfriend. Be like everyone else, don't be different, be a good girl.

God did I try to be a good girl.

I bought it all, lock, stock and at least four barrels! I wanted to stick in at school and get my Highers, to participate in all the concerts and plays but never, ever to show off (showing off is a hanging offence in Scotland). I wanted to be quiet in class and never be precocious or questioning of adults, to be nice to the boys and not fight with them or they wouldn't fancy you, to get to college and become a Primary teacher, get married to a lawyer, a doctor or someone with a better job than your dad, have a nice "bought house", a car and a couple of kids. I didn't want to be different, I wanted to be the same.

Maybe deep down there always was a desire to be me. Maybe something was put in the water in the sixties that made us object or take a different path from our allotted ones. The fact that other kids in my council estate were getting to college and university allowed dreams of other lives to emerge. (This was a time that you could actually get a grant to go to college unlike now.)

The writer and poet Liz Lochhead was brought up in the next street to me and always seemed like a totally exotic figure in her long coats, mini skirts, fabby shoes— all the gear. When she passed our gate on her way to Art School in the metropolis that was Glasgow, we couldn't believe that she was really a poet and that we knew her wee sister too!

[*Note on acceptable behaviour of families of a "turn"*. The only people who are allowed to be unbearable and brag about you are your parents. Brothers and sisters aren't or they will be perceived as being jealous so they must be humble and always happy for you. Distant relatives are allowed to boast and brag, usually when completely pished in a dive in Fauldhouse, because they can make up much better stories about you than the immediate family can, and they don't even have to pretend to like you. These tend to be the family members that the tabloids get to speak to when a tragedy hits your life, or even when an earthquake happens in South America and they want to know your opinion on it. It is great to know that the drunk uncle in Broxburn who hasn't seen you since you were four will be on hand to give that accurate, up to the minute comment.]

The first step to the other world was education and that generally meant Glasgow. Although the city was only 15 miles away it was like another planet to us. Special days had to be set aside to go there and you went for the day. It took an hour and a half by bus, so you set off at 9am, had lunch and came back home about 6pm, if you were lucky.

But growing up "nice" and desperately trying to be a good girl for everyone else was more important to me than anything else. Rebellion was for everyone else, I wanted to be liked and accepted where I was. That has remained with me all my life. What has changed is that now I want that acceptance on my own terms or not at all. Therein lies the struggle.

While I tried desperately to be like everyone else, I was actually surrounded by a world that was changing fast and forcing me to change with it. Lots of my peers were going to college because they could now afford to, sights were set high and wide and certain restrictions were relaxed. It was very confusing.

*　　*　　*　　*

The four-in-a-block house that we were brought up in was like a cross-section of a typical Lanarkshire community at that time.

The family who lived below us were wonderful. I've always thought that if you were to write a sketch about an archetypal Scots family of the late fifties in Scotland, then it would have been them. Great kindness and warmth, pancakes, scones and dumplings with silver sixpences made on an extremely regular basis.

Children were generally welcome and given goodies when they visited. Needless to say we visited often as all the grandchildren were of our age and we played all through the summer months with them. We had concerts, jumble sales, picnics up the metal raw burn.

No, it wasn't Suffolk or Devon, but to all of us we were the Famous Five. The coal bings in the distance were mountain ranges, and the farmer's fields across the road from us were as good as anything we read about in Enid Blyton.

As in any good childhood, the days went on forever and were generally full of some sort of adventure. We went to the pictures in Motherwell, or the swimming in Bellshill or Wishaw (brand new pool then with 3 diving dales). I still remember standing on the top dale for about

20 minutes willing myself to jump. Eventually I did and it was the most terrifying and exhilarating thing I've ever done. The feeling of terror before I jumped is the closest thing to how I feel on a first night—I know that there is no real choice but to jump, and it's all my own fault, since I decided to climb up those stairs in the first place! The only time I've come close to not making the jump and climbing back down the stairs was on the first night of *Shirley Valentine* when I came very near to telling the audience to go and collect their money because I just couldn't do it. Thankfully, I made a successful leap and didn't bellyflap!

Newarthill was actually quite rural then and we did walk up to the farm for eggs, though we hated going for a chicken because the farmer just went out into the shed and strangled it. Walking home with a newly strangled chicken in your bag gives new meaning to the phrase "free range".

Anyway, back to the downstairs neighbours. They were wonderful—a huge extended family headed by the matriarch, Mrs Maxwell. She was in her sixties by then and was quite deaf although the grandchildren believed it was selective. You could find her hearing very sharp if you gave her any quiet cheek—she either lip-read brilliantly or turned her hearing aid up a bit. (I think it was the latter since occasionally when any particularly juicy bit of gossip was being discussed, we would hear a loud wailing and screeching of feedback as she scrambled to adjust the volume and clear the wax from her ears!)

She was a real family friend and a godsend for my mother in a new home with three young daughters. She helped look after us on many an occasion, although her deafness could occasionally be a problem. Once, my mother left my then nine-month-old baby sister Diane with her. When she came up to relieve my mum the baby was asleep, and mum told her she'd be back in a couple of hours and that Di should just sleep. Mrs M. duly checked and said baby was asleep. Later, the baby awoke, in no distress apart from a full nappy, and when no one appeared to change her she decided to put her hand in her nappy and use what she found there to do some drawing. My mother returned to a bedroom covered in Jimmy Boyle type expressionistic paintings—critically panned as shite!

The family downstairs were close and had great family parties. Lots of drink, lots of songs and topped by Mr Maxwell's recitations of 'The Road to Ballochmyle' or 'Tam O' Shanter'. This was loyal Burns Territory—all very bewildering to me. I'd never heard of Burns, but in that mining community the ability to sing or recite Burns was enough to elevate you to God-like status. . . .

Talking of God brings us to their immediate neighbours on the ground floor. God, did they have God. They were all members, prominent boss-type members, of the Wee Free church. They ran the local Gospel Hall and wandered the village of a Sunday evening in a pack of around twenty preaching the word. Even as eight-year-olds we found this fascinating and really, really funny. We would follow them around finding the spectacle of open air preaching quite amazing and loving it if the preacher got very loud and angry and carried away with himself. Of course it was always a man who spoke. The women were visible and very noticeable because they said little, made the tea and were never allowed to cut their hair. Some of them had hair that trailed on the ground, but they always had to wear it tied up in a bun. We all went as children to their Sunday School, which was generally excruciating, though they did have the best songs, good evangelical tub-thumping stuff that made you feel great if you sung them dead loud. But the sermons were full of hell and damnation, which to a 9-year-old seemed no worse than having to sit through the service itself. Although we all went (the children that is, my dad was/is agnostic and generally worked overtime on a Sunday and my mum was a lapsed Catholic having married outside the faith), mum and dad were mistaken if they thought that our interest in Sunday school was spiritual. Only later did they discover that our desire to attend was due to the bar of Dairy Milk that was handed to each child as they left the hall. Ever since then, chocolate has been a great spiritual theme in my life. . . .

We played with the grandchildren of the God squad and were fascinated by the length of the 9-year-old's hair and by the fact that they were not allowed to have or watch TV. They were not allowed to play on the Sabbath and I remember seeing the faces of the children at the window on summer nights, watching us and dying to get out of their best clothes and run free. I still think it was cruel and so, so repressive for all concerned, particularly the women and children. 'Twas ever thus.

Our next-door neighbours, the Grahams, were a hugely artistic family. They were bright, they painted, played instruments and sang, the teenage daughters were pretty and trendy and played Stones and Beatles records, as well as singing all the words to Hamish Imlach's 'Cod Liver Oil and the Orange Juice' and various Burns tunes as well.

They were my heroes. I had a huge crush on Ross who played guitar and sang. I desperately wanted to be one of the girls who talked of going to Art college or becoming teachers. They helped open my eyes to the possibilities and excitements of that big world beyond Motherwell.

All of these people helped form and confuse me. On the one hand you could have nothing better than a large loving family who all lived a stone's throw from each other, but there were great opportunities and other lives to be lived out in the big world. I attempted to fulfil all of those desires and I think have gained in certain ways and lost in others. But in general, as I survey the surrounding landscape, I am truly blessed at being able to have much of both lives. I will never be that housewife and mother that somewhere locked in my brain I think I should be. But I do have a husband I love (who was a teacher—see, a better job than my dad!) and two beautiful daughters. I hoover, make beds, do laundry and trek around Safeway with a moaning toddler turning blue when she's refused a packet of mini eggs! I will also never be that Hollywood type that swans around cocktail parties or the pop star that is chauffeured around in huge limos and feted by all. But I do have many advantages because of the little fame I have and compared to working as a domestic in a hospital I have a glamorous and privileged life.

Trying to be a good girl and not offend the men has in many ways failed miserably—I started to blow it early on due to the fact that I could never keep my mouth shut. It is my greatest attribute and my greatest failing all at the same time. It has brought me many friends—and made me many enemies too. I wish I could say that I always speak from the heart and make myself out to be a heroine of sorts, but I can't. I do genuinely try to say what I feel and believe, having thought, discussed and deliberated over things, but that doesn't stop me from talking out of my arse sometimes—for which I am sorry.

The combination of where I was brought up, my family and my dreams are what has brought me to this point in my life. My stage show, *Elaine With Attitude*, was written as an attempt by me to come to terms with the road I found myself on. A road that in many ways I stumbled upon due to some talent but also at a time when the genius that was and is Billy Connolly made it acceptable to go on TV and tour the country with a working-class accent.

I suppose in my own way I was inspired to do and say what I wanted because of him. I didn't realise that being the wrong sex in the world of comedy would be such a difficult barrier to cross but I decided to be brave and take to the road—which is how I ended up doing what I'm doing. If people want to listen then I'm glad, if they don't I'll sell my house!

1

THE SHOW

I had never written before. My years in the BBC Comedy Unit had left me feeling that writers were a breed apart (well actually they are) and that I would never be able to write properly, be a real writer. You had to be really tortured, bitter and twisted about what directors and producers were doing to your work and always feel unappreciated and underpaid! Actually now that I think about it I am perfectly qualified to be a writer. I guess I just never had the bottle.

In all the years on *Naked Video*, I'd never once even suggested a sketch—I was too afraid of sitting around that table in the rehearsal room and hearing it being torn apart. My idea of hell! I had been hired as an actor and to be truthful, I was delighted at that and never ever thought that I had any writing talent. No one discouraged me or encouraged me. I had too much respect and reverence for writers and didn't feel that I had any right to assume that I could do anything that they could do. It's a classic cocktail of fear, inferiority and gender. Writers were nice middle-class people who'd been to Oxbridge. Of course that is not completely true, it was just my assumption and prejudice (although a look at the backgrounds of many of the writers on TV nationally 10 years ago would have confirmed my prejudice). I was just scared.

I met George McKechnie at a function somewhere. He was at that time the editor of the *Evening Times* in Glasgow. Now I've always had quite an amusing caustic mouth and for some reason George liked the cut of my jib. I liked him too. He has a great, gruff bear-like manner which many of his staff were scared of but I just liked him. He has all the stuff that I love about Scottish men. Intelligent, sharp, funny, occasionally brusque, obstinate, belligerent and egocentric but underneath a heart overflowing with emotion and compassion. I got all of that the first time I met him and basically he liked me because I was cheeky!

Anyway, he phoned me up and asked me to come and see him in his big posh office, and tried to convince me that I could write. I kept saying that I couldn't do it, but I left the office having said that I would give it a go.

I sat in front of the typewriter practically crying. I approached it like a college essay and handed it in like I was handing in an exam paper. I found out weeks later that Russell Kyle (a great guy) the features editor was dreading my stuff coming in. Apparently, they'd done some stuff with other "celebs" and they always had to doctor their contributions, so he thought that George had handed him another nightmare wrapped up as a good idea. So I handed it in and they came back saying that they quite liked it but I sounded too much like a journalist! They wanted me to sound like Elaine C. Smith. Eh? Who was she? I didn't realise that I sounded like anything, but I realise now that they wanted me to write the way that I talk. That is very hard to do after years in education, having your essays penalised for being too subjective. I worked on it and gave it a bit more of a voice and they printed it. It was a scary experience especially when readers wrote in on the subject, whatever it was. Dear God, that meant that people actually read it. The only comfort was that by about 10 o'clock folk would be wrapping their chips in it. I carried on writing for a couple of months and my articles were alright but didn't set the heather alight.

Dealing with what sub-editors can do was a learning

experience, mainly realising that they rarely read what you write and put any old headline across it next to the stupid photie!!! I wrote one piece about the tragedy of one aspect of Mr Gorbachov's Perestroika. I felt it a crying shame that one of the first things that was reinstated in the Soviet Union were beauty contests just as the West were finally getting rid of them. What was the headline? 'Niet, niet says Gorby!' Next to a huge bikini-clad model in the photo. They had obviously not read my piece and thought that I was saying great, let's have beauty contests!

I stopped writing for the *Times* to have a baby and then started up again when Katie was about six weeks old. I wrote straight from the heart about the madness that ensued after having a baby, that nobody ever told you the truth about how sore your nipples would be, that you couldn't sit down without the aid of a rubber ring and if you were out of your pyjamas by 4 o'clock you felt like you had just won the Olympic pentathlon! For the first time in my life I was so knackered that I didn't care if anyone liked it. I just spoke as me. The phone rang immediately the copy hit Russell's desk and he said "That's it. That's you, for the first time you've cracked it." I was bewildered and couldn't believe the amount of mail I received from women agreeing with me. I had found my voice on the page.

However, I still didn't think that I could write. I was an

opinionated columnist who had a name thanks to TV. Even though I continued to do pieces for magazines and newspapers, I wasn't a writer. I'm still not.

That is why sitting down at a typewriter in January 1996 to write *Elaine With Attitude* was so terrifying. The wonderful Paul Bassett had asked me to do a show for Mayfest and I liked the idea of a big, unapologetic show with a ten-piece band, linked with bits of my life. I had toured a smaller version of this a few years before and discovered that audiences liked my chat between songs, which got longer each night! I had never got that show quite right and I always wanted to try and do a bigger, better version of it. But this time I had to be disciplined and write it all down and see whether anyone thought it was funny. It was a nightmare. Like childbirth without the epidural.

I had a brilliant midwife though in Kate Donnelly. A wonderful woman, great actress, writer and all-round good girl. From the first time I went to Kate's house and stood up in her living room and read my stuff, to the moment I walked onstage in front of two thousand people at the King's in Glasgow she was there. She helped me be confident, to phrase and time things, she criticised, laughed, cried. I couldn't have asked for better. She also gave me some of my favourite lines!

I realised that I had to go out there and use the writing

and the show as a kind of therapy. I didn't set out to do that but it happened that way. I was at a point in my life where I needed to try and make sense of all that was happening to me. I was a public figure, people spoke to me all the time as if they knew me intimately. The preconceived notions that people had about me, the information they had gathered from newspapers and TV, the fact that my life was now like living in a goldfish bowl was weird. Any actor has dreams of fame and fortune due to their massive ego, but few handle that fame very well. I am no exception. I am better adjusted and pragmatic now, but even a couple of years ago I was confused about the journey I found myself on. Writing it all down and being funny about it really helped. People responded because I think I was prepared to reveal a bit about my fears, phobias and general neuroses—it made them feel normal.

Many people find a display of personal neurosis too revealing, but I find it liberating. It helps you deal with the damage and chaos and makes you view it from a distance, allowing you to stand back, take a good look at yourself and laugh. Someone doing it in front of an audience is also liberating for the audience. I once asked Billy Connolly if damage had played a big part in his comedy and he said yes, absolutely. He said that he needed to make sense of the madness of his early life with the crazy women he was brought up with and telling those stories about it is liberating. To demonstrate this he told me about the trauma of living with women who knitted all the time, and the madness of waking up in the morning with a scratchy, knitted sweater on when you had gone to bed in a vest and pants! Obviously these women thought that trying a jumper on a small boy in the middle of the night when he was asleep just to see if it fitted was an okay thing to do! They didn't think that it might terrify a six-year-old to wake up with a hairy skin, wondering what kind of disease had occurred during the night? All the stories of hand knitted balaclavas with one ear in the wrong place, giving the wearer a somewhat disturbed look if he tried to make the ears fit in the right place, were born out of the real pain and confusion of a young boy trying to make sense of the world he was living in. (Hard to do when your gloves on a string are too short and putting your hands in raises your shoulders to Quasimodo-like proportions.) Just telling the world and laughing about it really helps you to understand it.

But there are some things that have to remain locked away. People often make the mistake with loud, open individuals of thinking that they have no privacy or boundaries. They do, but the things that they share are generally good for us all to share.

So I did it. I wrote and performed this piece of my life,

Elaine With Attitude, and chose what I wanted to share and work out. It was the first real thing I'd ever written. If you saw the show, you might recognise some of the characters as they appear in this book, and if you didn't it shouldn't stop you from following the story. It seemed like a good idea at the time. . . .

2

THE BOWELS OPEN . . .

Mayfest 1996. Old Fruitmarket, Glasgow . . . packed . . . a very deep breath and . . . blackout . . . walk onstage to the mike. Now . . . just talk to the audience . . .

"I am 39 years of age, YES . . . 39! I know everyone thinks that I am 50 and 15 stone, but I'm not. Get it into your heads that it is simply wonderful bloody acting that I can transform myself from this gorgeous young thing you see before you into the harridan with dubious taste in clothes and hair that you are so familiar with. I know you are all dumbfounded. I hear you whispering 'But that can't be her she's beautiful!' Yes, ladies and gents it's me alright. So you're not saying that, you're saying 'who the hell is that, I booked to see Barbara Dickson.' Well, tough—you're here now . . ."

It never changes. Just before I come onstage (after I've managed to be dragged out of the loo), as I do that very long walk from the dressing room to the stage and then the agonising wait until the audience get themselves comfy, I think "What a ridiculous way to make a living!!!! Why do I do this to myself? What is it that I need to prove? Grow up, go and get a proper job, get some computer skills and stop this nonsense now."

Acting and performing is a strange way to make a living and I must say that I only really feel this bad for the first few performances, after that it is much more enjoyable and becomes just like going to your work, except that 1800 people are watching you! Weird. Becoming known as a particular character is very strange because people start to believe that you are that character and hate it when you attempt to get out of your box. Is that a Scottish thing? "Get back in your box hen, and don't try to do anything else!"

Now, if I was in Hollywood, I would be applauded for wearing hacket clothes, a bad wig and no make-up. I'd be hailed as a great character actress. I mean, Robert De Niro puts on weight and a daft wig and bad make-up, and he gets nominated for an Oscar. What do I get? Two guys hanging out of a bread van shouting "Hello Mary Doll" on the way past. . . . It's not fair is it? Could Robert De Niro play Mary Nesbitt? Well he probably could, actually, and he'd fit right in in Govan. "Ho, are youse talking to me? Are *youse* talking to *me*?"

*   *   *   *

This whole fame thing does have a strange effect on us though. Not, you understand, that I think that I'm Demi Moore (although funnily enough a lot of people have said that I'm her spit, and I have to admit that we do have very similar ankles). I am very well aware that I am a big tadpole in a very small pond, but I have had to accept that in certain quarters I am well known.

It always amazes me that people are interested in all the details of my life. My mum's friend works in an office in Hamilton and apparently when a picture appeared of me with my living room in the background they were all more interested in the background than in me. It was all "Is that Elaine's living room? Is it the rust carpet that she's got? That's a lovely lampshade that"! But I am just as bad. I sit in the hairdressers reading *Hello*, or the Govan equivalent *Hawyou*, and I find myself thinking "God, I thought Michelle Pfeiffer would have had a nicer coffee table than that."

I'm fascinated by what it is that drives people to want to be famous in the first place. In this age of celebrity and of people being famous for simply being famous, I wonder what secret ingredient completes the cocktail of drive and ambition.

What makes somebody want to be famous in the first place? The root of it all appears to be in the family.

Well, if you read up on things about famous folk then they usually come from pretty weird families, not your average, if there is such a thing. Down through history your great painters, writers, composers had quite a bit of the mad bastard in them.

Now while I'm not saying that it is entirely necessary to have a bamstick family to become a performer or a great artist or simply to be famous, it does seem to help. Though it is not always the case. A lot of people with crazy, bamstick families become taxi drivers instead! But as a general rule a liberal dose of madness in the family, a modicum of talent, and a huge ego coupled with massive self-doubt, seem to be the lethal ingredients necessary for the heady cocktail of fame.

Mind you, if that's the case the whole of Scotland should be famous, since we all seem to have those ingredients at our fingertips—particularly those well known big-heads, the Glaswegians. Maybe that's why the pubs are so full in Glasgow, they're either drowning their sorrows because they are not famous or pretending that they are to the few folk that will listen!

So I had to take a careful look at myself. How have I ended up performing for a living?

Yes, it's all there! The ego, the insecurity, a bit of talent and a lot of luck.

But what about the family? Oh yes . . . yes, it's all there . . . the madness and the mayhem. So where do we start to lay the blame for all this? Well, the parents of course! We have to start with the parents. . . .

*   *   *   *

My mother is great. She is kind, warm, a super gran, champion baby-sitter, good at her job as a sales person, and could worry for Scotland. She is mental, though no more than her friends or the majority of her family—and I include myself in that. She also has the ability to talk underwater. A great skill and one which you'll note that I have inherited!

She has a fabulous memory, (another thing I've inherited, for which I thank her—a good memory is a huge asset if you are an actor) and an ability to go off at a tangent that is world class. My mum sells new houses and is great at it because she cares about the deal that people get and understands how much it means to them when they are buying a home for the first or second time. She is friendly and gets information freely from people— I am always amazed at the things they tell her. My mother no sooner starts a conversation with her customers than she has their life story and is giving them advice on everything from carpet fitters to the collapse of the Russian rouble.

My mum phones almost every day just to check that everything is alright, and if she has nothing else to do then you are there for the duration—wherever her thought processes and her stream of consciousness take you to.

She'll start with "How are things? How are the girls? Katie get to school alright? How many nappies has Hannah done so far? Only four, is she a bit constipated? Maybe you should take her to the doctor (it is necessary in every conversation for her to find something to worry about, particularly with her grandchildren). . . . Oh well if you think she's alright. . . . I just had Mrs Wilson in there— she's a lovely woman. Remember I told you that she bought one of my two-bedrooms? Mind you they are good flats, a bargain too. Well they were giving carpets, blinds, choice of bathroom, kitchen with fully integrated appliances and choice of tiles and units all included in the price. I think she chose the festoons actually, though I wasn't overkeen myself, but it's her choice, she's got to live with them, but I would say she got a snip. Anyway, she came in this morning with a wee box of chocolates for me—Milk Tray, the very chocolates that I can't stand, but I didn't like to say, though a wee Belgian chocolate would have been better—anyway it was awful nice of her. It was just a thank you for helping her out when she moved in. Well I felt it was hard for her leaving that big house in Bothwell and coming here, although she says that she loves it. Mind you, it must be a relief to be in her own place—she's had some time of it. Well, remember I told you about the husband going off with that young hairdresser, that boy that was a junior in Irvine Rusk. Oh, big scandal . . . and that beautiful house, too, I used to admire it when I drove past and you always think that it would be marvellous to live there and that the people would be happy in it but there you go . . . now some footballer has bought it, who is it again . . . Ally van Hoodoink or something . . . now I only know that cos I was in Marks in Hamilton the other day and I met wee Angela . . . I was thinking of getting the Little Mermaid pyjamas for Hannah, do you think she'll like them? Anyway I met Angela . . . remember her? She bought the studio flat off me after she got dumped at the altar by the Egyptian doctor that worked up in Law? Well, believe it or not, she is now married to him and has got a house in East Kilbride. See, you never know the minute do you? I was never that keen on him (I thought he was a bit shifty—

a bit too charming, you never know with doctors) but she loved him, she used to come in for a chat and I would hear all her woes—I felt that sorry for her so I am delighted for her. She looks so happy and she's expecting too, only five months but by God she's big, I'd have said she was seven months and she looks to be carrying a bit too much fluid round her ankles and her face is like a Hallowe'en cake, though that could just have been too much blusher under those lights in Marks, they don't do very much for you at the best of times . . . but it's great news eh? Anyway she told me that her sister is very friendly with that footballer's wife . . . Ally whatever . . . apparently they go to some step class in Uddingston together . . . and that they bought the house that Mrs Wilson lived in. Small world, eh? Mrs Wilson couldn't believe that when I told her because she was in such a state at the time she didn't really care who bought it and because her daughter is a lawyer she was dealing with all the conveyancing. Her daughter—a very nice girl, very bright although not the best dress sense in the world, doesn't make the best of herself—she came out here one day and I kid you not she had a blue suit on with a brown bag and black shoes, now there's no need for that is there. I felt like saying 'Oh come on hen you could have matched that a wee bit better' and her a lawyer too, what would her clients think if they noticed that? I mean, up in the high court with a bag that doesn't match, it'd make me think twice about hiring her . . . but it's true what they say, intelligence doesn't buy taste . . . though she is very good to her mother. . . ."

Well, by this time I have been round Safeway, done my ironing and cooked the tea and my mother hasn't drawn a breath yet.

My dad on the other hand was quieter, well he would have to be, but when he spoke we all had to listen. In the sixties your dad was still the boss and the house was run to suit his working hours. Everything had to be ready for him coming home for dinner. There was none of this "Oh we'll just send out for a curry or get fish suppers," mainly because they were too expensive—fish suppers were what you got as a treat when you went on holiday. My dad was also a great cook and insisted on good grub, none of this pie and chips routine, we had to have soup or stew or mince or chicken and always with veg. Veg was a big deal—no sweets if you didn't eat your veg. He taught my mum to cook, as she hadn't a clue when they first married, and stories abounded of her efforts to boil an egg or the time that she left the kettle on the gas so long that when she went in to investigate the burning smell all that was left was the handle! But she learned and became a really good cook, all to dad's specifications.

So mealtimes were a big deal and this was usually when the kids got a grilling or a lecture from dad on whatever took his fancy. He had an incredible ability for tangential chat and flights of fancy which we desperately tried to follow, with little success. We occasionally attempted to ask him stuff of a more mundane nature, but he was usually in the midst of a monologue about MacPherson struts or the fuel consumption of an average two-litre engine. For years we believed it was his superior technical brain whizzing through important data that could not be halted, but finally realised that he just wasn't listening. When dad decided to go off on one of his techno trips the weans had to go with him, whether we wanted to or not.

His work always seemed exciting and I think that it gave me a determination not to be stuck in the house with kids, but to be in a job where you were out there in the world, having a laugh and earning money.

My dad was an engineer and, like many of the men of his generation from the Central Belt, actually believed that everyone in the world was as interested in the internal workings of the combustion engine and the construction of the Forth Road Bridge as he was. Although he had three daughters and no sons, that did not deter him, and we were treated to a nightly talk on what happened at work, followed by his thoughts on the contribution of ball bearings to Western Civilisation, which, in his opinion, was immense.

A typical teatime chat would go something like this:

"Well, that's some job I'm working on the now."

"Is it dad?"

"Oh aye, ye see there's a lot of debate in the work about the ability of certain metals that can and should be used for an outside job and their ability to withstand corrosion."

"Is there dad?"

"Oh yes. Ye see, there are a few of the guys believe that we should use tungsten."

"The hardest metal known to mankind, dad?"

"Correct doll, very good, you were obviously paying attention the other night when I was telling you about strong metals. Of course, tungsten is the hardest metal at the moment, but twenty years from now it may not be, an that, but let's just say for argument's sake that it is. . . . Anyway, big Charlie was saying . . ."

"Dad, me and my boyfriend were wanting to go away on holiday together . . ."

"It's funny you know, because Charlie is no expert on metals at the best of times . . ."

"I know we've only been going out for seven weeks but he's really nice and my mum says . . ."

"In fact the other day we were talking about . . ."

"My mum says that you have to make the decision because she thinks 14 is too young to go on holiday with him . . ."

"Well, Charlie starts talking about desert islands and

Robinson Crusoe, and I says that was not a desert island. Do you know that there are actually only seven desert islands in the whole world? And I mean desert and I mean island. No vegetation. None of this Robinson Crusoe stuff, that was not a desert island. I mean there was Man Friday for a start . . ."

"We'd only be going camping dad . . ."

"Naw, a desert island is exactly that, a desert and an island . . . no more . . . no less. And most people don't grasp that . . ."

"I'll just ask my mum."

*　　*　　*　　*

Quite a combination, eh? Not quite psychos, but enough to set a girl on the road to getting noticed. But enough of the trauma and pain and on with the tale. All I'll say now is that the years of therapy, the prozac and an occasional blow with a very large mallet have all played their part in getting me onstage.

And we haven't even met the rest of the family and friends yet . . .

Apart from my family there are two other major factors in my personal psychosis and they are (a) that I was brought up in Lanarkshire, and (b) that I was brought up in the 1970s. A deadly combination.

You see if you are brought up in a city then you have a sense of belonging. If you live in Edinburgh then you have an identity, you come from the capital city—or Inverness or Dundee, you have a sense of belonging, of who you are supposed to be.

The Glaswegian has a huge sense of identity, the biggest ego in the land and the swagger to match. That's why they bug everyone so much, because they think they're great, swaggering about going "Ah'm fae Glesca. Ahm are byreway." (Though I do have to give the Glaswegians great credit for their language skills and abilities—anyone who can use a phrase twice in the one sentence and afford it different meanings as in "EH, byreway, byreway" is something of a master.) But, even if you live in Castlemilk or Haghill, you are still a Glaswegian and you swagger about thinking that you're great (it's the rest of us that think you look like an egit). Unfortunately, if you come from Motherwell, the only thing you've got to swagger about is that at least it's not Coatbridge!

I suppose if you live in Coatbridge you can swagger about the fact that it isn't Kilsyth or Bonnyrigg or, even worse, Broxburn. Oh come on, we've all done it. We've all sat on the M8 driving home approaching Broxburn and thought "Eh, I think I'll just put the locks in the car doors down." Well you can hear it can't you? The banjos playing in the distance. Dee, dee dee dee, dee dee dee dee dee.

Heh, it's Deliverance country up there, too many people with the one eyebrow for my liking if you catch my drift. . . .

Actually most performers in Scotland are from outside Glasgow, but we all pretend to be Glaswegians, so that folk in the Pavilion will like us—well you know what Glaswegians are like, they string you up if they think you're fae the country.

The fact that I was brought up in the seventies had a big effect. I found a photo the other day and I could not believe it. There I was with the blazer, the Oxford bags, the smock top, the platforms and the Farrah Fawcett flick-outs, the Led Zeppelin III album under my arm with the cover out the way to show how hip I was (the Chicory Tip album was around the back). I thought that I was gorgeous. Tell me, how could a generation that thought we had got it so right get it so wrong?

Yet, my best memories of New Year come from the seventies. That was when we still knew how to celebrate it properly. There was still a big family party with enough money to spare on food and drink, although not enough to go abroad or out to some hotel. It just wasn't done then. This was the first generation of people in the steel towns who all had permanent work and there was great joy and comfort in that fact alone. They were also of a generation that knew how to enjoy themselves together. So New Year was still a very big deal.

*   *   *   *

The parties in our house on Hogmanay were great, a real occasion and I think I got a lot of my love of performing from them. I can explain it no other way. We didn't go to the theatre, there wasn't one. I had never met anyone in showbusiness or had any idea that a career in entertainment was even an option. I had none of the traditional showbiz family connections or Oxbridge pals running the RSC or the National. I didn't even know that these places existed. All I knew were the performances of my aunts and uncles and that when they sang we listened and applauded and when they told stories or jokes we all laughed.

No party was complete in our house without a big pot of vegetable soup and the chicken curry that my dad made. Now my dad was a great cook, but I've never tasted another curry like it, full of sultanas and fruit and explosive. I'm sure there were a few ball bearings thrown in as the secret ingredient. We all thought it was totally exotic—well it was the seventies.

Getting ready for the party was like preparing for an opening night. My mother would run around like a blue arsed fly, usually cursing the fact that she always ended up having to have the party and that she had all the work to do. She would be saying "How the hell is it always us, I always get left with it all, no other bugger takes their turn" etc. Of course when the relatives arrive she's as nice as ninepence, with the pan-loaf voice, saying "Hello, come in, lovely to see you, och it's no bother, we love having a party."

I loved the time just before everybody arrived. The telly on, the house different because all the furniture was moved to allow more seats in and only the coffee table in the middle with the crisps and the peanuts on it (this would be moved later when the dancing started, due to the fact that one year Auntie Betty had backflipped over it during a jiving session and didn't realise that she had done her back in until she woke up in agony late on New Year's Day).

Anyway, the purple swirly carpet was hoovered, the purple swirly suite and curtains were looking lovely, the purple wall with the three others white were all immaculate. What a room! I am telling you, when you walked into our living room you had to hold onto the door jambs because you kept getting terrible vertigo, it was so swirly.

Drugs? We didnae need drugs! One can of super lager, a walk into the living room and we were away.

So we'd have the curry bubbling away, the Trini Lopez records on and in the centre of the room we had . . . the Magicoal!

Now Magicoal was amazing because it was basically a wee bit of moulded plastic made to look like coal and placed over a red bulb. There was no heat from it, but my mother was convinced that when it wasn't on the room was cold. So it had to be on all the time, so that we could get the wee glow. The Magicoal was the centre-piece of the fire surround—a marvellous contraption. Well, you see the fashion then was to rip out the nice Victorian fireplace and replace it with a fake mahogany surround with little shelves for the porcelain ornaments and, on some models, little leatherette doors down the bottom.

So we had the glow on full blast, (complete with white bulb covered inventively with my mothers red lipstick as the red one had blown and the shops were shut).

In the hall, my dad had been out with the paintbrush and had re-emulsioned the artex.

A great invention artex, you just put a coat of emulsion on and it was as good as new, the only problems came when you wanted to put up wallpaper and then you had to practically demolish your house to get it off the walls. We had that Mr Whippy, Mount Vesuvius swirly effect. You couldn't wear a cardigan in our house because if it caught on the pointy bits you were stuck there for hours. There was a guy along the road from us who actually artexed his doors. It was a two man lift to get into the living room and we kept seeing his weans with loads of plasters on and realised that they kept running into the artex!

So we are all prepared. The house is ready. The family arrive.

Now everybody is on their best behaviour and all the hatchets are buried for the moment because it is New Year and they've not had enough to drink yet.

The aunties are commenting on everything from the new curtains to the lovely new glasses.

"That's a lovely wee tumbler that Stella? Here that's a beautiful wee Capo di Monti figure that—here did you get that in Goldbergs?"

My Auntie Magrit and Uncle Peter arrive and we all wait to see what kind of mood she is in. We have been forewarned that things are not good as Peter, who has a tendency to go "a wee message" that takes him via various local hostelries, which in turn prevents him from returning home for two days, is currently in the dog-house. So, suffice it to say Magrit has a face like fizz!

Though Magrit had a tendency to always have a face like fizz—she was obviously born that way—Peter had never managed to help straighten it, in fact he had made it worse. They were one of those couples who had been together for years and nobody knew why.

Peter was trying to worm his way back, but she was having none of it. He had that false cheeriness in his voice asking "D'ye want a wee whisky Magrit?" The look she gave him would have turned milk as Magrit said very menacingly "Shove it!" We all kept our distance and tiptoed gently around them waiting for the volcano to erupt. Peter, meanwhile, headed into the kitchen to where the bar was set up and all the men were naturally gathered.

I was in my teens at this time and singing in a band in Glasgow and my parents told me to bring a couple of pals. So a couple of the guys in the band turned up for the free drink and the food.

Zeke the drummer was black.

Now, in Newarthill, in 1976, there were *niente* black people.

So, Zeke walking into our living room was a showstopper. You know when the baddie walks in to the saloon in a western and there's a sudden hush, well just for a second that is what happened, then of course everybody starts falling over themselves to greet him and show that him being black makes no difference to them, except the only thing they can talk about is the fact that he's black. Wee Isa the neighbour is in there first. She speaks dead slow:

—*Hello son, I'm Isa, how long have you been here, son?*
—*About 10 minutes.*
—*Naw, I mean how long have you been in our land?*

I was mortified. Zeke of course had lived in Glasgow for quite a while, so was rather used to the well-intentioned racism of the populace. It never ceases to amaze me that people feel that because a person is another colour then it is only right and proper that you confront it head on and mention it. They don't think that this is racist because they are simply stating a fact. (They do, however, understand how it feels when as a Scot on holiday they are consistently referred to as Jock and that the first question asked when they open their mouth is "Are you Scottish?" When you answer "Yes" there then follows a stream of very tiring assumptions about kilts, haggis etc.)

And so in 1976, although they were completely welcoming of Zeke, they did treat him like a prize exhibit.

My aunties were around him rubbing his head and saying things like "Oh he's got beautiful teeth, hint he?" "Mind you they've aw got that han't they?"

Fortunately Zeke is saved by the doorbell. All you can hear is a Manchester accent and a voice saying . . .

"Well, about 4 o'clock I said to her I says, well why don't we just jump into the new Rover and drive up to see the Jocks in Jockland, I mean this is their time of year so let's give them a nice surprise! Well here we are!" As they walk into the living room we hear Derek saying "Hello everyone. Well, where are your kilts, where are your haggis?" The family loathed him on sight but tried very hard to be the warm hospitable Scots. Who were they? Yes, you've guessed it. The couple that they met in Majorca, that they exchanged addresses with, thinking that they would never see them again, have taken up the offer of the Scots New Year. . . . This is a couple who could bore for England, not that their nationality had anything to do with it because they could bore for any nation.

The family had met Derek and Michelle while on holiday in Majorca, well actually Peter and Magrit had met him and then inflicted them on the rest.

Uncle Peter had a terrible hangover and had been in search of the local "Farmacia". They found one but unfortunately the guy only spoke Spanish. This did not deter Peter and he proceeded thus:

"Eh, excusie Señor. My heedo is bursto. Gonnie gie us sumhin furrit?"

The guy looked blank. Peter repeated it slower this time and enunciating as he went.

"EH, excuusiee señor. My heedo (pointing wildly at head and miming) is bursto (explosive movements and arm waving). Gonnie gie us sumhin furrit?"

The guy still looks blank.

At this Auntie Magrit loses her patience and says "Oh fur Christ's sake can ye no see the boy disnae understand? I'll speak to him."

She walks forward and smiles sweetly and in best pan-loaf voice says:

"Excuse moi, s'il vous plait. Pardon moi por favor! His heedio ella burstio. Kin you gee him simhing furrit?"

Total blank stare from said guy.

Enter Derek and wife who have a smattering of Spanish and rescue the situation and get the drugs, which makes Peter extremely grateful, who then invites him back to the hotel for a drink. Insists in fact. The family spend a few hours listening to Derek, the scrap metal dealer, recount numerous unfunny tales of his wealthy life and they realise that they have met a man in search of a punchline who rarely sticks his hand in his pocket for a drink but always takes one in everyone else's round—not popular!

Peter can't get rid of him and when they finally do, after two days of hiding in cafes and saying that they are going to one pub and then going to another, they leave for Manchester. Not before Peter presses my parents' address into Derek's hand saying "Now, if you're ever in Scotland come and see us. You should come at the New Year— you'll have a wonderful time!" Never for a moment expecting them to turn up. But they did.

So my pal Zeke was off the hook. Well, let's face it. If there is a choice between winding up a black guy or winding up an English guy, well then there is no contest is there?

The family are all trying to be nice, but throughout the night, Derek continues winding everyone up. During the sing-song he slags people thinking its funny. As wee Isa is giving her all in 'My Ain Folk' he's saying "Hey, who let the cat in? You call that singing?" It's going down like a lead balloon. We can hear Uncle Peter giving it "Ah'm goonie lamp that bastard—ah am." Well we all know the rules. You never, ever talk while the singers are singing. Wan singer, wan song. The best of order. Anyone transgressing will be chastised. It's as bad as trying to walk through the Orange Walk, it's not done and you will be in grave danger of being battered over the head with one of the purely ornamental ceremonial hammers!

The curry is over, the show has started. This is my favourite bit of the evening. This is where I did my apprenticeship. . . .

*　　　*　　　*　　　*

There was a showlike quality to all this and I noticed early on that the good singers, or those who considered themselves to be good singers, never ever sang first. They always had to be coaxed, then stood out of the way looking superior as everyone else was singing. But the duffers, those that warbled on forever, couldn't wait to get singing. They were in like a shot! So, there was a definite pecking order and I soon realised that I did not want to be a duffer, I wanted to be top of the bill.

So, Isa starts with the usual 'My Ain Folk', during the course of which everybody is greeting and pretending they know the words, as is usual with most Scots songs. We pretend that we love them and in a way we do, but at parties we have the Scots songs first so that we can move swiftly on to the songs we really love—usually a Frank Sinatra.

So at least we can all join in with the last line with Isa as we all sing "Back hame in Bonnie Scotland, Wi' ma ain folk", followed by much crying and cheering. Then comes more community singing with that well-known classic, "Dee, deedle dee da dee dee, Dee dee da de da dee da, dee dee da dee dee dee dee. (Everyone loudly) . . . Scotland the Brave!"

Then we get my Uncle Peter. Now Peter, as we all know, gets a hard time from Magrit and ninety-nine times out of a hundred she wins, but on Hogmanay (or Mahogany as Derek insists on calling it) Peter is allowed his moment of glory. Everyone loves it and he always sings the same song directed at Magrit and accompanied by a particularly gallus dance. He takes the floor and starts . . .

Well there's too many Chiefs and not enough Indians
*   around this house,*
Baby I'm tired of this old game we play called cat and
*   mouse*
If you don't give just a little bit more,
We're both gonna lose the race,
Coz, there's too many Chiefs and not enough Indians
*   around this place.*

Roars of approval and sideways glances at Magrit reveal a fixed grin and a look that says "Aye, very good. Just remember it's me you're coming hame wi' the night." My Auntie Magrit then gets her turn, and of course she sings the Shirley Bassey, the torch song. There's always a Shirley Bassey—usually punctuated with withering sideways looks at my Uncle Peter.

She sits glass in hand and sings in a very Lanarkshire accent (though to her she sounds like Shirley . . .)

Ayee, Ayee who have nuhing,
Ayee, ayee who have no one
Adore youoo and waant you so,

Ah'm just a no one with nuhing to give you but oh
Ayee lo-ove youuuuu!!!

Everyone applauds respectfully because they are feart to do otherwise. . . .

Then comes the top of the bill, my cousin Kate. Now every family has their really good singer and ours was Kate, and there was always a wee bit of a show when she sang. She never sang at the start of the night, all the duffers got their chance first. Well it wouldn't be fair if they had to come after her because she always got the biggest cheer. So we get a great rendition of 'Lipstick On Your Collar'.

Now, after Kate, the only ones who will sing are the ones who think that they are great singers, or who are completely steamin'.

And that very person has just walked into our living room. Our neighbour Donald. You know just by watching him that he is going to wake up on New Year's Day with the one sore leg, due to the fact that only one leg is actually moving. He stands pointing at no one in particular, with one leg constantly stepping in and out as if was actually trying to walk somewhere and not quite making it. He is constantly saying "Naw in a minute, in a minute . . . Jim, Stella, Kate . . . in a minute . . ." but he never gets past that sentence. It's all nods and winks and pointing until he eventually gives forth with a huge:

"AND NOW THE END IS NEAR . . ."

But unfortunately for us it isnae near. It goes on forever. . . .

So naturally, folk get fed up and start to chat and ignore him but he keeps going, oblivious to the fact that things are getting very heated with Derek and the boys in the corner. You can hear things like "Well if you could get some decent players then maybe Scotland would beat England, but I don't see it ever happening. You don't have the brains, you lot and the Irish should stick to drinking and digging roads" etc etc.

All the women are in the kitchen having the fight that all women seem to have—you know, the I'll wash the dishes Stella you go and sit down, you've been on your feet all day. . . . No it's my house I'll do it etc etc.

My dad is explaining the internal workings of the combustion engine to my boyfriend saying:

"Well I have actually built a couple of combustion engines in the past myself, in fact I've got one down in the garage the now. I'd take you down to see it but everybody else would want to come and the garage is too wee. I'll take you down the morra."

Old Isa is greeting in the other corner with various

arms around her as she bawls "Billy, Billy—he was . . . the best wee dug that you could wish fur, he would just look up wi the big eyes . . . as if to say . . . MAMMIE!"

Then the rammy starts. Peter says, "Right, that is it. I've sat here all night listening to that whining English bastard put us doon, chat up my wife, talk absolute shite and now, now he slaps her on the arse. Right, outside, OUTSIDE . . . "

—BONG (bell ringing in the distance)

—BONG

Peter is saying "eh . . . what . . ."

—BONG

"Oh eh, sorry Derek," proffers hand. "Eh, eh, Happy New Year . . . all the very best. . . . "

3

THE REAL STORY

My parents are a union between a lower middle-class convent school Catholic from Bellshill and a relatively poor working-class Proddy from Holytown. Not much in that I hear you say, but you have to set the scene in the dark bigotry of 1950s Lanarkshire. There was a community madness at this time that could result in instances like my mother having been married for five years and pregnant with me, finding herself being harangued by her parish priest for "carrying a bastard child" on the main street in Motherwell! These attitudes must have pervaded any mixed marriage at the time and for many years to come.

How can sanity prevail when a young girl gets married and the church excommunicates her just because the man she loves isn't a Catholic? So we've got massive family and religious guilt before the marriage even gets off the ground. My poor mother—all that to live with at the age of 19.

The groom (my dad) may not have been a Catholic but he was, however, a really hard worker and a great dad, so eventually the family came around, but there was never a particularly relaxed atmosphere around my mother's family gatherings. It was never bad or ugly, just odd. Even as a 4-year-old I could detect that something wasn't quite right when we were all together, but I didn't find out why for years.

My dad's family had very different and more immediate concerns, as there were ten children, some still at home, and very little money to go around.

When I used to go to my Gran Smith's I had a feeling of being overwhelmed by all the people. There was always a huge pot of soup, my gran in a Maw Broon type apron, my papa sitting in a blue pullover, a shelpit thin figure, smoking Senior Service surrounded by all his adult children and, at that point, 23 grandchildren and some great grandchildren on the way. I loved it but just wished that my grandparents would recognise me and remember my name. I can't blame them. I would have been demented, with all those grandkids around. But I was still the oldest daughter and the centre of my parents' world and found it hard to believe that I wasn't the centre of everyone else's. The necessary narcissism of a 4-year-old. Somewhere it must have locked in—the need to be noticed in a crowd.

I was, however, noticed very much by the other grandparents as I was the first grandchild on their side, so the contrast was quite stark. I was constantly given sweets and money by an elegant, erudite and extremely witty Winston Churchill lookalike who was my grandfather. The amounts varied according to how much alcohol he had consumed—and it was usually rather a lot. This was a great source of amusement and bewilderment to me. Why was papa crying while listening to John McCormack singing 'The Kerry Dancing', and why did he keep giving me half a crown?

I found out later that my papa was from Ireland and a relative of the Papal Count that was John McCormack (for the uninitiated he was/is one of the finest tenors ever produced by Ireland. He made many, many recordings, toured the world singing and even sung in Hollywood in the 1920s—a family hero). So my papa's tears about the life he had lost in Ireland were brought on by the beautiful lilting version of 'The Kerry Dancing' and several large whiskies. Here was this elegant intelligent Irishman living in Lanarkshire with six kids in a council house finding that his career could go no further in the steel towns due to the fact that he was a Catholic. He sought solace in the bottle and in the driving ambition for his children to succeed. They did with four going on to university and his only son becoming a doctor—but I'm sure that all of his children and his wife would have preferred a more sober and much happier father.

But to me he was wonderful. He was incredibly funny, I mean really funny. A man of great and real wit. My mum had many a run-in with him as she grew up but still maintains that there has never been anyone funnier. He was also apparently legendary in his kindness and generosity. If any of his family needed a place to stay, he was the first to say come to us. The problem was that when they arrived with bags and belongings he could only bear to stay in the house for short periods, as the combination of both visitors and children became too much for him to stand. I'm sure that like many an individual faced with six children or more, he craved a bit of solace and peace, and for men the easy option was the pub. Women did not have that option and my poor grandmother had to deal with it all, but she did, and made a good job of it. I think gran survived all this because she was an avid reader and was apparently able to read a book while merry hell broke loose around her—usually in the shape of an assault course being made out of the bedroom furniture with all six kids balanced precariously around the room!

There was also a great deal of grief involved. I don't think that papa ever got over losing his son Kevin, who was only six months old when he died in his arms. People go on living but they never get over these things. They have a great and devastating effect on the entire family. I think it was especially difficult for my uncle Jim who, as the only remaining son, had a lot to prove and live up to. The younger children also had to deal with a different sort of father than the older ones had experienced—a father who drank a lot and was full of grief and anger.

But I don't want to get all maudlin and *Angela's Ashes* on you! As a child, I just enjoyed myself and only realised that things were amiss as I grew up. This was not the usual West of Scotland poverty-stricken family. This was a lower middle-class, well-read, well-educated, devout Catholic family. If there was any poverty it was very genteel. I always thought of them as posher than us. They turned the TV off when visitors arrived and only had it on when they wanted to watch a particular programme. Weird! The house had paintings and books and the table was always set for dinner with a tablecloth.

My gran was full of kindness and knowledge. She was a very intelligent woman who hailed from Dalkeith and did not marry until she was in her late twenties. If she hadn't married papa, I don't think that she would have married at all. She loved him very much. I think she would have been a bit of a bluestocking in another life. She was tall (5 foot 8) and very elegant. I miss her to this day. She taught me to knit, to set tables properly and she took me to mass but never ever pushed her religion or the fact that I was different. She had great patience and instilled in me a love of books that I have carried through life. Reading will always be my solace.

The older you get the more you appreciate all the other people that were around as you grew up. In your twenties you go around rejecting and lampooning all the aunties and uncles. You end up at family weddings and get embarrassed at everyone reminding you of what you did as a kid and it seems a natural process to want to live as far away from them as you can to help assert your new life. But now I can see all the warmth and kindness that I was surrounded by as well.

Not only did some of my dad's family live near us, we all went on holiday together. Bridlington, Morecambe, Rhyl and Whitley Bay—we went there about five years running. These resorts didn't know what had hit them, but generally we had a ball. We drove down in convoy with my dad in charge—until people rebelled and took their own routes. But we would have meeting points along the way. Everyone else would have pieces and a flask of tea, but not us. We would all be starving and stealing our cousins' sandwiches, while my dad would unload the car to produce the folding picnic table and folding chairs that were only ever used on the journey down, because nobody wanted a picnic on the way back—they just wanted home.

So he humped this yellow formica effort all that way just so he could sit in a lay-by near Carlisle. He would then produce the wee gas stove, the sausage, egg, bacon, black pudding and potato scones and start frying, while all the time giving everyone approximate times of arrival, distance covered so far, and the estimated cooking time of a fried egg on a calor gas stove! We just wanted a piece and a drink. But no, we had to sit there with the table set and eat a full breakfast. We were always last to arrive.

So if you were ever en route to Whitley Bay and saw some folk sitting in a lay-by, with a full breakfast on a picnic table, and you found yourself laughing and pointing and saying "Look at those eejits!", just remember that those eejits were us!

Louise and Diane (my two wee sisters) would fight for the entire journey (which in those days could be as long as six or seven hours). My parents were demented by the time we got there. My father always got particularly stressed with us shouting and screaming or having a carry-on on the back seat. At times we had to sit in silence so dad could concentrate on the difficult driving and road conditions which of course we didn't give a toss about. He would get very worried about anything going wrong with the car and was always listening out for suspicious clonks or bangs. On one occasion my sister Diane opened a bottle of lemonade in the back seat, letting out a loud hiss. We immediately found ourselves crossing two lanes of the motorway onto the hard shoulder and Dad then got out to investigate a suspected flat tyre. To describe his reaction on finding out that said hiss was from a lemonade bottle as mild and congenial would be a vast understatement. The rest of the journey was spent in silence with dire warnings of no holiday money ringing in our ears. We were also banned from bringing any fizzy juice into the car for life.

We would meet up with Uncle Andy (dad's younger brother—the spit of Gene Kelly) and Aunt Frances (the kindest woman in the world) and their four kids (my favourite cousins). Then came the Conners who were called Auntie May (my surrogate mother) and Uncle Tommy (the real Dean Martin) but were in actual fact no relation. They had three girls as well so we played great guns with them! Then came Auntie Rena and Uncle Nick (dad's older sister and her husband) and their only daughter Kate. She was my big cousin and a bit of a hero of mine. Kate was tough, said what she thought, was married to a wonderful man (Jim), had two lovely kids and was a great singer. If we went to clubs or parties, Kate was always up there and I wanted to be like her.

One of the first times I ever got up and sang professionally was in Cullercoats in Whitley Bay. Its one and only claim to fame was that The Animals and Alan Price had started there. I didn't care. I just knew that when I sung 'Will You Still Love Me Tomorrow' at the age of fifteen, they loved me, and that was enough for me.

It was that summer that I felt I could match my big cousin. We both sang that night. My family hadn't actually noticed that I could sing until quite recently. I must have been thirteen and although I had sung in school and stuff, I had never really passed the family test. I sang at a party in my mum's living room (where else?) and there was a sort of stunned silence from the relatives when they realised that I could actually sing. So I daresay that the rivalry between Kate and I started then. It must have been difficult for her having been the family star to suddenly have this young pup snapping at her heels. We did remain close and friends, although we inevitably drifted apart a bit when I went to drama school. But I loved her and have never quite got over her early death from cancer at only 42. Her children and her husband are a credit to her, and I often feel that a lot of my drive comes from her. I named my first daughter Kate.

*   *   *   *

So from these humble theatrical beginnings a performer grew. I learnt a lot from all those characters and experiences in my family but didn't connect them with acting. They were just our family and like many families we relied on each other to provide the entertainment for each other.

I don't think many of our family and friends ever went to the theatre—if they did it was for something special. It was never to see plays. They were strictly for the upper and middle-classes, as generally the stories concerned the lives and loves of those classes and had very little relevance to the men and women who worked in the mines and steelworks of Lanarkshire. If Bob Hope or Danny Kaye or Morecambe and Wise or Shirley Bassey or some other big movie or television star was on in a theatre they would all want to go because these people meant more to them than a Strindberg or an Ibsen play. If they did go to the King's or the Pavilion, it was for a Variety show.

My only experience of theatre before I entered the rarified atmosphere of drama school was of a Variety show hosted by the Alexander Brothers and starring wonderful people like John Grieve and Roddy Macmillan. I found the whole experience rather bewildering but do remember laughing at Roddy as a drunk man trying to get in the front door of his house and singing 'Nobody's

Child' along with TOM AND JACK! (those showbiz legends that are the Alexander Brothers—and they're from Wishaw). A great night out for an 11-year-old. When I look at my own kids and how *au fait* they are with the theatre, the staff, the backstage and all of that, I can't quite believe the difference between our lives.

Cinema was the big love. For most of my childhood, all the entertainment references around me were from films. Every Saturday morning we caught the bus at half past eight clutching our precious pocket money and went to the pictures in Motherwell. I was only six. There were two cinemas in Motherwell in 1964, the Rex and the Odeon. They ran a Saturday Club for kids. They were a riot. Trying to watch your favourite Enid Blyton serial surrounded by screaming mental weans who were either going to the toilet, going for ice cream or being thrown out by torch wielding attendants for bad behaviour was an education. I loved it. The worst thing I ever did there was to meet up with my cousin John and his pals, buy sixpence worth of rotten fruit and chuck it at the screen when a baddie came on. My cousin was thrown out, I started to cry, pleading innocence and saying "He made me do it!" I was let off—he was banned for life! The difference in the cinema when a picture came on that we all loved was remarkable. There was silence because the characters were ones we could identify with. These were usually in American films. British films were too posh and too boring. That's why Doris Day had such an effect on me. I was desperate to be her. These films transported you to another world full of hope and light and promise.

To this day I would still rather go and see a movie than a play. That is not because I don't like the theatre. I do. A good night out at the theatre, whether Shakespeare or Billy Connolly, is a fabulous experience. I've just had too many rotten nights in the theatre over the years, so as a punter I feel the safest bet for a good story and good acting is the pictures.

Like everyone else, I had my heroes when I was growing up and the first time I saw Doris Day riding in on the Deadwood Stage, I was in love. I wanted to be that woman. I wanted to be a tomboy that could shoot and ride horses and sing and dance. I wanted to wear a suede trouser suit and still look fab in dresses. Every girl's dream is that people will see the beauty in her even though she is different and lives life her own way and in the end you get to marry Wild Bill Hickcock who loves you warts and all. Perfect. . . .

Because there was nowhere to go, nowhere to learn or to put all that energy, I lost myself in the romance of the movies on TV. We all loved those movies where the plain, unknown but secretly very talented wee girl was plucked from the Chorus line and given the lead role when Mr.

Zeigfeld said, "That girl on the left, she's the one I want." I kept waiting for that to happen to me in Motherwell. There I would be, onstage in the Gilbert and Sullivan musical at Braidhurst High, and in would walk this big producer who would shout "Yep, she's the one—the wee dumpy one on the left with the loud voice and the big chest—I'll make her a star!"

Surely that's how it would happen? . . . Doris Day here I come . . . NOT!

THE BEST DAYS OF OUR LIVES

I could never ever confess to my friends or family that I wanted to be Doris. It was not done. Any notion of grandness or of being different was stamped out at a very early age. Where I came from, no one wanted to be an actor. That was stupid and not of the real world. Go and get a real job, like teaching or nursing. An actor? Who do you think you are? You think yer big jist cos you can sing a bit or act a bit or paint a bit don't ye? Stay here in the pot of lobsters with us and if you try and escape we'll pull you back in. It is this type of mentality that beats up young guys because they've got a trial with Celtic. Envy, fear of the unknown, their own thwarted dreams and ambitions.

One of my favourite episodes of *Rab C. Nesbitt* is the one when it is discovered that Burney has a gift for painting. Mary is delighted but Rab is eaten up with jealousy of his own son because he never got a chance to discover if he had any gifts. He was just condemned from birth to being factory fodder.

Maybe the harshness of working-class life is what gave me that push and I should be grateful for it. But I see such a freedom in my own children's lives because theatre, music, books and art are seen as a normal part of their lives and not something different. When I was growing up, peer group pressure and the surrounding landscape determined what you could like or dislike in life and anyone who deviated was a snob or posh—a terrible crime.

So announcing in Primary 2 that you wanted to be a singer or an actress would have guaranteed you years of taunting and ridicule. I desperately wanted to be liked and to be seen as normal. Even to this day I find it hard to deal with being different—I certainly couldn't at the age of five and definitely not at fifteen.

So I tried to be normal and be like everyone else.

But I could sing and play the piano, which was just about acceptable because you got into the school concerts, and the teachers seemed to approve of it so that was alright. It was like the kids who were good runners or swimmers. It was alright up to a point, but to confess that you wanted to really make something of your talent—to play for Rangers or swim in the Olympics—was not recommended.

My first audition was for my primary school headmaster. We'll call him Mr Brown in case any of his family want to sue me. He was a horrible, cruel man who ruled by fear and punishment. I doubt if he would even be allowed to teach now, but in 1967 a headmaster was a law unto himself.

He had an ability to humiliate that was second to none. We had some really tough, hard boys in our school but Mr Brown could completely break them down.

If a boy (only boys) misbehaved, he used to haul them out of their seats by the ears or nose, get them to kneel in front of him as he sat down pulling their head between his legs. He would then proceed to sing a song while drumming on their behinds with his hands. This was done in front of the class and depending on the offence it could be a quick chorus of a song or a full three verses. I have never forgotten the red faces of the hardest boys or the tears rolling down their faces on the way back to their desks. It was awful. Of course at nine or ten you just accept it and only later do you realise what a bizarre and obviously sexual game was going on.

So this was the man that I had to audition for. I was terrified. For some reason rather than sing 'Ye Banks and Braes' like the others, I chose to sing the Beatles 'Norwegian Wood' simply because I thought it was a beautiful song. The class all giggled as I got to the line "and then she said it's time for bed". Despite the fact that I did not sing a Burns song, I got into the concert. But the headmaster would get his revenge.

Until this point I had been in the top three in the class (only ever getting true praise from the parents if I was first—therein lie the seeds of my competitive nature and the drive to succeed) but when we were taught by the headmaster I dropped to 13th. I was completely bored, demotivated and disillusioned. Until this point I had been very enthusiastic about school, although they never allowed enough talking and gossiping for my liking, but this man killed it. I hated him and he hated me. Before we went to the big school our parents were called in to talk about our prospects.

From Newarthill Primary you had a choice of schools. The brains were to go to Dalziell High, the alrights and nearly brainies went to Bellshill Academy and the duffers and delinquents went to Braidhurst High in Motherwell. All the family's hopes were pinned on me getting into Dalziell, but on my present showing I was headed for Bellshill. My mother was very upset by this and asked the

Heedie if he thought I wasn't bright. He said on the contrary that I was very bright but (then came the body blow) that I was the most insolent and disobedient child that he had ever had the misfortune to teach. That blew my cover I can tell you. I walked into our living room to find a mother in tears and a father with the crabbitest face I have ever seen. But there was no recourse, no one would listen to a ten-year-old. I wanted to shout that he was cruel and vicious and boring and to tell them what he did to the boys, but I didn't know if it was wrong. He was an adult and therefore must be obeyed and respected just for being an adult.

I got a huge lecture about being lazy and was told that I was going to end up as a bus conductress if I was lucky because they could at least count. It was a complete sherricking.

My mum has since confessed that she thought the Head was an awful man and that she wanted to punch his lights out in the office when he said all that about me, but in those days headmasters had to be respected and listened to even if they were bamsticks.

I was chastened and worked harder and I was saved from the ignominy of not going to the brainbox school by the Comprehensive system. Thank God for it!

Zoning had arrived and regardless of your abilities you were all sent to the one school. We were bussed to

Braidhurst High in Forgewood (At that time Motherwell's equivalent of Easterhouse) and we were terrified.

5

THE BRAIDHURST YEARS

I was frightened and excited all at the same time. The blessed relief of being away from the mad headmaster, a chance to begin afresh, and the real start of growing up. The terror came from all the stories about the school itself— that it was in a really tough area and that there were running gangfights in the playground. We were only from a wee village and although we had tough local guys who ran around in gangs they weren't the same as the knife wielding thugs that we were led to believe ran the school. In reality, at the end of the sixties there had been a few battles but nothing compared to some areas of Glasgow. I was actually more afraid of the tough girls from other primary schools who thought that you were a snob if you had a schoolbag.

The school was a tough school from the disciplinary point of view. The then headmaster was very much of the old school, so everyone had to wear a uniform, be on time and an assembly was held every morning. We were belted daily as a matter of course for any minor misdemeanour and as first years we were terrified of certain teachers, especially if they wore gowns. This was 1970 and the school was only a few years old, a typical example of comprehensive design—lots of glass, wood and concrete. Teachers wearing gowns did not seem to fit in with the trendy design of the school. Female teachers were not allowed to wear trousers. Any female pupil wearing make-up or deviations from the uniform would be belted or sent home. (I was told by one teacher when I was found wearing eye make-up en route to assembly to "Go immediately and wash that massacre off your face".)

Attitudes to women were very rigid. The great Calvinist, masonic, anal retentive was well established in Motherwell and women were at the bottom of the heap—next to a few Catholics! Even in the late 80s I was shocked to find that female teachers were still not allowed to wear trousers.

Thanks to my Primary school report, I was not put into the top class. Even though it was a comprehensive, we were streamed into classes based on our supposed abilities. Top were the brainies, then the nearly brainies, then the saveables and then the duffers. I was in the nearly brainies which was a disappointment because I didn't get to do Latin—which meant my hopes of being a doctor like Uncle Jim were dashed. My mum was upset as she had been good at Latin at school and would have liked her daughter to have been a doctor just to prove to the family that she was a success after all. I felt her disappointment and to be frank I was miffed because I knew that I was as brainy as some of the people from my school who were in the top classes. I set about rectifying the situation by trying to learn Latin myself from my friend's books. After a week and a half I had to admit defeat and concentrate on the other subjects. I discovered an ability to come out fighting when the chips were down and I worked really hard and was eventually moved up into the brainy stream at the end of second year, having reached the top three in most subjects.

Except maths. I hated maths. We had one of those teachers who thought if you asked a question then you were being insolent. When I finally plucked up the courage to ask why (a+b)=c, I was put out of the class and told that I had far too much extrovert energy. I had the cheek to ask him what that meant and he told me to go and look it up in the dictionary. When I got home I asked my mum what it meant and she said that it meant I was a show-off. Well fair enough, but I just thought I was being inquisitive. Another lesson I should take on board regarding people's misinterpretation of your intentions. Maybe he just saw something that I didn't. He may have been a rubbish maths teacher, but he could obviously spot a show-off at a hundred paces.

Schools are not designed, or mine certainly wasn't, to deal with anyone creative or different. I just wanted to be a good pupil and to be liked, but my actions didn't seem to get that message across. As I went through school and became more confident in my surroundings I felt that I had the right to ask questions and that that would be encouraged. Unfortunately, children who were nearly brainy asking questions was interpreted as insolence and cheek. "I never ever meant it that way, honest sur, it jist came oot."

I did eventually discover somewhere that I could express my creativity, and that was in music. I had been going to piano lessons for years and though not guaranteed to stimulate the mind of a teenager, I did like the fact that I could read music. That gave me some brownie points. And the attitude of some of the "hard" lassies changed during our first week in music when we had to sing in front of the teacher. We all had to take a couple of lines of the 'Four Marys' and sing it solo. I was very nervous, but when it came to my bit I just belted it out. That was it, instant approval. Smithie could sing!

I was also now in the school choir, which was led by two very nice teachers, Mrs Johnson and Mr Cameron P. Merriweather (there's a Proddy name if ever there was one). They started me on the road to acting, though I am sure that they didn't know that at the time. The choir led on to the school opera. Every year they put on a Gilbert and Sullivan, and even then I doubted the relevance of such entertainment in Forgewood. I would have preferred *Annie Get Your Gun* or *Calamity Jane*, but in school you are at the mercy of what the teachers like, and Mr Merriweather liked G&S, so we were stuck with it. I hated all the girly soprano singing "Gaily tripping" and all that malarky, so I spent much of my time taking the piss— until one very wise member of staff, Mr Hunter, intervened. A wonderful Techie teacher who actually liked his pupils, he had spotted me early on in my school career and had christened me "Basher"—after an incident where I bashed a guy when he tried to put his hand up my pal's skirt. He liked the cut of my jib and thought that I was funny, so he suggested in rehearsals that I would be better as a WPC with the police in *The Pirates of Penzance*. At last, my first comedy role. The idea was a simple one in that I would be the only WPC in a long line of policemen singing the old tarantara song, and I would have a wee first-year boy as my new recruit who would get everything wrong. Really just a variation of the old Variety Maw, Paw and Wean sketch, but I didn't know that when I was fourteen. It brought the house down and I got a special mention in the *Motherwell Times*. Even my mother said I was funny!

I was belted quite a lot during my first couple of years, usually for talking. (Hard to believe, eh? I was obviously just practising for the future!) I am a total supporter of banning the belt. I saw great cruelty inflicted on children for nothing, depending on the whim of the teacher. Respect was given to teachers if they could "draw the belt", while perfectly good teachers were ridiculed if they couldn't. I saw boys given more than six of the best, hit around the body with a belt by the mental Geography teacher, and a wrist split open because our young French teacher enjoyed using his full weight while belting 13-year-old girls. Really good teachers rarely used the belt because they could control children without using violence. When I became a teacher myself, I never used the belt in three years and I had to deal with some pretty tough kids. I know how difficult and challenging and bloody exhausting teaching is, and the temptation to belt the life out of third-year bams is a very real one, but we all know that if you have to resort to violence then you have failed.

So I tried hard and like many kids I excelled at the subjects I liked—English, History, Music. Generally, our enjoyment of other subjects depended on whether or not we liked the teacher. If we didn't, we were bored rigid, and most mischief happens when kids are bored. Initially I was too scared to say boo, but by third year I thought I was the cat's pyjamas. I was made a prefect. I was in the brainy class doing seven O Grades, I was in the choir and getting parts in the school operas and I was getting a lot of interest from boys. T Rex were at the top of the charts. Life was mine for the taking. . . .

The problem was that in the next two years I forgot that I would have to study. Well I did a bit, and for the first few exams I got through and did well in the subjects that I liked. But more and more my interests were outside school. Discos, boys, records, boys, pals, boys. From the age of thirteen I don't think I was ever without a boyfriend—not because I was gorgeous, but because I was relatively pretty (well it was Motherwell), and because I was a laugh and gabbed so they didn't need to try and make conversation. I had a great time and had many great loves and passions and many broken hearts. But my head was the proverbial mince, and confirmation of that fact came when that doom-laden brown envelope dropped through the door. I had only passed three subjects out of seven, the three that I liked. My life was in ruins. The shame of it. The parents were far from pleased, but, worse, I had to go back to the school and face all the brains who were staying on for highers with me and confess how badly I had done. Another lesson learned. Nothing comes without hard work.

But I faced it, took the patronising looks on the chin and got stuck in. I loved my fifth year. The teachers treated you like nearly-grown-ups, the work itself was more stimulating, and into my life came a wonderful teacher, Norrie Bissell. He taught my favourite subject, History. He encouraged us to take notes, like at college, and miracle of miracles, he *wanted* us to ask questions and when we did he didn't think that we were being cheeky. Amazing!

I was becoming more friendly with the girls that until then I had seen as a bit swotty and uncool and discovered that they weren't. I had always wanted to look like Elaine Porte—she was very pretty and brainy. Elizabeth Brown turned out to be a good laugh, while Marion Mcvey and Anna Dow (who I had always liked) turned out to be great pals too. We had a brilliant time and a different world opened up, that of great female pals. I began to realise that I didn't need to have a boyfriend to be complete and that there was a great big world out there beyond Newarthill. These were all girls who wanted to go to college or university and I realised that I could go too. Peer group pressure is such a powerful thing and I no longer needed to please the pals who just wanted to go looking for guys all the time.

I had started to sing with my cousins John and Jim in

a band around various local clubs. We were pretty rotten but we thought we were brilliant, and all the more so because we got a Saturday afternoon gig in The Motherwell Trades and Labour Club and were paid 50p each. I had only really started doing it because of another girl in my class who was a really good singer. We used to harmonise at the drop of a hat, although she was a much better singer than me and I always felt sure that she would be a big star. I was just enjoying myself. But she was very shy and didn't really come out of herself onstage. As a woman in the lavvies of a club once told her, "You're a good singer hen but you should be mair like your pal, she's got aw the actions—she's selling it." Like I say, I was just enjoying myself. . . .

By the time I hit fifth year I was in a folk band singing James Taylor/Joni Mitchell type songs and after a lot of practice I realised that I actually had a voice. It was a great time for music and I started to learn a lot about performing without even realising it. You learn what not to do first, usually from the disastrous gigs—of which there are many. When I think of the poor punters who had to sit through it, I want to phone them up and give them their money back!

Anyway, I was working hard, passed all my highers and O grades and I had a good time. I had a steady boyfriend. Life was good.

I left Braidhurst in 1975 feeling that I had achieved something. I had been a far from perfect pupil but I had come out the other end alright thanks to teachers like the ones I've mentioned and the ones that I still occasionally see like Dorothy Adams and Miss Kelly—who hasn't changed a bit, and I still can't call her anything but Miss Kelly.

THESPDOM

Sitting bored out of my brains in a maths class in my fourth year at Braidhurst, I started gabbing (of course) to a pal about what she was going to do when she left. Christine Crichton was her name and I haven't seen her for many years, but I owe her a great deal as she is partly responsible for the path that I am now on. Christine was a lovely girl who was quiet, diligent and brainy. My opposite! Like me, she sang and was in the school opera. Anyway, she confessed to me that she also went to elocution lessons, but I promised not to let on because that sort of thing, along with playing the violin, could be a hanging offence if the rest of the class got wind of it.

She said that she would like to be a teacher when she left. I asked her what subject and she said Speech and Drama. Eh? I did not know that such a thing existed. She told me that many schools now had teachers who taught drama, and that was what she really wanted to do. A seed was planted. Over the next few weeks I became more and more interested, constantly asking Christine how you trained etc, and she offered to get me some info, which she did.

It seemed perfect. I had always wanted to teach, although I didn't know what subject—I just wanted to teach children and work in a school. Of course my head was full of all the great things that I would achieve, loosely based on not being like the majority of the teachers that I had experienced. I went to my English teacher and asked him if he thought teaching drama would be a good idea. He seemed to think that it was ideal, given my involvement in school shows.

I had recently "triumphed" at a parent teacher do, when I was asked by Miss Adams if I could write something that would allow the acts in the concert to be more than people just walking on after each other. So, with no experience whatsoever, I went off and wrote a play about a group of kids putting on a concert to raise funds for a youth club and all the acts that turned up for auditions to be in the show. It was a simple, fairly unoriginal idea but at sixteen I thought it was the most original thing ever done! I was in it, of course, and I sang a James Taylor song, 'Fire and Rain', which was a bit risqué compared to *The Pirates of Penzance*. I was accompanied by Mrs Johnson on the pianoforte. She was great, although I don't think she had a clue who James Taylor was, or that it was a song about someone committing suicide.

Anyway we were a smash.

So, I got a bit of a reputation for the drama and all that, which my English teacher thought was great. So, he sent off for all the application forms and I got an audition in July of 1975. School had broken up. I had no intention of going back. I just wanted to pass my exams and get out into the world. But I had a feeling that this drama school thing would be good, especially if I could become a teacher at the end of it.

Of course, like many people I thought it would just be teaching acting all day and be great fun. I had no idea that it would be used by most schools as a way to occupy remedial and difficult children. They had replaced raffia and lap bags with art, music and drama. The only subjects that really mattered were ones that you could get a traditional qualification in. The powers that be, particularly in the West of Scotland, had no idea of the benefits to the whole child as a person that creative subjects can give them.

In order to get into the teaching course, you had to have the usual Highers etc, but you also had to go for an audition. I really thought that this was going to be like an interview, and didn't even smell a rat when they asked me to prepare a poem and a piece from a book.

I went in blind and didn't know what had hit me.

I suppose I did feel that I was talented. I could sing, play the piano and act a wee bit. I thought I could dance a bit because I could Harlem Shuffle around the Heathery Bar in Wishaw, but I had never been to a dance class in my life. The shock when I walked into the waiting room at the Royal Scottish Academy of Music and Drama was immense. I was surrounded by girls in leotards, with wraparound skirts and chignons, all doing stretching exercises. They were all speaking in what I would term "posh" accents and they all seemed to know each other. I felt like I had walked into a parallel universe. No one in Motherwell that I knew had even seen a leotard never mind worn one! It was not a vital fashion accessory up Brandon Street. I had, of course, turned up in my best gear. Being 1975, I was wearing the customary clumpy six-inch platform shoes along with the three-piece suit with wide lapels, waistcoat, high-waisted trousers that flared out loon-like over my shoes right down to the ground. I thought that I was gorgeous. When I saw all these other women I felt that I had a neon sign flashing above my head saying "LOWLIFE". Just to make things worse, they were all obviously *au fait* with the procedure and I overheard someone say that it was their third or fourth attempt to get in! What? I thought this was going to be a dawdle, a wee interview, read a poem, they'd discover my natural talented fabness and that would be that. What was happening? The panic rose and I was trying to work out if I had time to have the runs or not when my name was called.

I headed into what was called the Improvisation audition. I had no idea what that meant. The two people on the panel (one was the infamous actor and movement lecturer Pete Lincoln) put me at ease and explained that it simply meant that they would ask me to do things or put me into situations to see how I would act and react. Fair enough, I thought, I can do that. They then asked me to remove my jacket and shoes. Eh? That would spoil the look of the suit not to mention the fact that I was about to shrink by six inches and have my trousers flapping around my ankles. I must have tripped half a dozen times.

Not only that but they then asked me to do the most ridiculous things I had ever heard of. I stood in the middle of the floor, trousers trailing, and one of them said:

"Now, could you climb an imaginary rope ladder?"

"Eh, yes," I said. Pause.

"Well would you do it for us?"

"What, now?"

"Yes, now."

Oh my god . . . I wanted to laugh in their faces and give it "Aye, Right", but something told me that that would not go down well. If I had said "Hey what's this got to do with acting?" I think I might have blown my chances. I learnt my first lesson in acting. If a director tells you to do something that you think is really stupid then take a deep breath and do it. They are the boss. Even if you feel scared, embarrassed or out of your depth. Just make an arse of yourself and hope it works. So I took a deep breath and climbed an imaginary rope ladder, I can't remember reaching the top but I felt like a complete arse. They didn't laugh out loud or faint so I must have been okay, but all I can think of now is the total tripe that poor old Pete Lincoln has had to sit through all these years, God bless him. . . .

Next I was asked to play at tennis with myself. In for a penny . . . but what an eejit! My first and only reaction was to try and be both players. Instead of standing on one side of the net and miming playing and hitting the ball back, I ran from one side of the net to the other, hitting the ball back over then running to catch it. I was bloody knackered! God knows what they thought I was doing. I have this picture of this whirling dervish with flapping troosers running from one end of an imaginary tennis court to another.

Last we had the bit of drama where I had to react as if I was in a burning building and trying to escape. Fine, I thought, and did a few feart looks and then ran out of the door. It was only when I was on the other side of the door that I realised that I should maybe have prolonged the acting a wee bit more. I had to knock and ask to get back in. They thanked me for coming and directed me to the next stage of the audition. Shoes in hand, I flapped off with as much of a flourish as I could muster. I felt like I was in a mental asylum.

Thankfully, the next part was singing and that passed without incident.

The final part was the readings and I did my recitation of Edwin Morgan's 'The Death of Marilyn Monroe'. This had been found for me by Mr King in my school's English department, as poetry was not really a strong suit of mine. Too many weeks spent on the 'Rime of the Ancient Mariner' in third year had put me right off. But I found Morgan's poem wonderful, so much so that I did not really believe that it was truly a poem. I loved it. I was then going to read a passage from *Dr Zhivago*, but I had made the fatal mistake of assuming that they would have a copy there. Guess what? They didn't. So I was handed a piece to read. By then it was all such a blur that I can't now remember what it was. I was in such a state that I had done it all wrong that I just blanked everything out. I do remember one of the panel reading a newspaper all the way through (apparently that was a ploy to freak us out and see how we coped). It was all awful and I was starting to feel like I had been hit by a truck. But I do remember making the panel laugh during the chat and telling a couple of stories about my stupidity and all that.

At least it was over. . . .

The journey home by train was a blur. I wanted to run up to complete strangers and say "Do you know what just happened to me? I had to climb an imaginary rope ladder and play at tennis with myself." I would have been carted away! I felt like I had been in an accident and suffered terrible trauma. What kind of thing is that to do to a 16-year-old from Newarthill.

I had been totally unprepared and couldn't believe that there was a whole section of the world that understood the language that was used in that building. It was a middle-class language of experience, sophistication and knowledge of which I had no part. It was like suddenly finding out that the world was round and not flat. I couldn't have felt more alien and isolated if I had landed on Mars.

Halfway home on the train, I started to find it funny.

And by the time I got into the house I was far enough away from the scene to tell the story of my day and have everyone in stitches. I've never been so glad to be home and among ma ain folk.

Two days later I got a letter from the RSAMD telling me that I had got in. I was stunned. I had been experiencing such relief at the prospect of rejection, because that would mean I could stay where I was and not have to enter that other world. The letter changed everything and, though I was bewildered as to why they picked me, I knew that I had to do it. My parents were delighted even though they weren't quite sure what the course was. The only thing that mattered was that I was going to be a teacher and that their daughter was going to college. A very big deal. I think that I was the first one of the Smiths ever to achieve that honour.

THE FIRST DAY OF THE REST
OF MY LIFE AND ALL THAT

When I think about my first day at college, I feel quite sorry for that wee girl of seventeen years and three weeks who set out at 7am. I intended to stay at home and travel in and out to Glasgow. Unfortunately, the First Year annexe was in the West End in Athole Gardens which meant that I had to get a bus to Motherwell, a train to Glasgow and the subway to Hillhead. Until then I didn't even know that the subway existed. My knowledge of Glasgow was limited to Argyle Street and C&A. I will never forget the feeling of nausea the first time I attempted to go down into the underground. I turned back twice because the smell was so awful. Finally, I forced myself down the stairs and boarded a train for Hillhead. As I walked into Byres Road, I could have been in another country.

I found the college and must have been very early for one of the few times in my life. We were greeted by the diminutive Grace Matchett. Tough as old boots with a heart of gold. To me she looked exotic, like a retired ballerina, and I know that Grace would find this description hilarious now but at the time she was the boss of first year and a force to be reckoned with. Naturally, in the state I was in, I was terrified of her.

I don't show fear in a normal way. When I laugh too loudly, or talk too much and too quickly, it's a sure sign that I am finding it difficult to cope. But to the world at large I just sound like someone very confident and loud. An empty vessel. I am sure that Grace and many of the students around me felt that I was like that. I've often described myself as rather anally explosive. Boundaries are things that I have had to learn—usually rather painfully too.

Generally though, people were lovely and I have made friendships that have lasted to this day. The delectable Irishwoman Gwen Atkinson and I have now been friends for 23 years. Which was a bit of a shock when we discovered it the other day. . . .

However, I did feel as if I had a sign round my neck that said "seventeen-year-old, working-class, Motherwell". There were people in my year who already had degrees, who had had fabulous jobs or just some experience of the world. I was a baby. I therefore set about just trying to fit in and be like everyone else—the old feelings that I had in childhood about being the same. But I couldn't be. Dear God, there were a couple of girls in my year who dressed for dinner! I felt like I was drowning for the entire first term. Any confidence that I originally had was gone and although I could swank about a bit at home because I was at college, the truth was that I have never felt so miserable in my life.

Somewhere in the second term I started to make friends and one day I was taken aside by Boss Grace and told that she was very pleased with my progress. She said that she had been a bit worried about me at the start but was now very pleased. I felt like she had given me a million pounds.

*   *   *   *

Even though we were in the middle of Glasgow, we could have been anywhere. It was really strange that an institution based in a major Scottish city had only two Scottish lecturers and did not teach the history of Scottish theatre. Everything we were taught was about the Greeks, the Russians and English theatre. I didn't know if any real theatre even existed in Scotland. It was looked down upon as being substandard and not "real" theatre. Billy Connolly may have been packing them in, 7:84 and Hector Macmillan's *The Sash* might have had them queuing around the block, *The Slab Boys* and *Benny Lynch* might have been packing them in in Edinburgh, but to us they didn't exist. That was punters theatre and it was looked down on. Ibsen, Chekov and Shakespeare—now that was considered to be real theatre. I am no philistine and I know great writing when I see it and love these great playwrights. (One of the most memorable nights in my first year was watching a production of *The Three Sisters* with Jennifer Black and Phyllis Logan. I had never been so moved by a play.) But I can't bear snobbery and that is all it was and is. If entertainers are putting on stuff that audiences adore then that has a right to be called art too. It is just different. It may not last the centuries, but for that moment in time it is bringing joy and entertainment to an audience and that is every bit as valid as great art. But not at drama school in 1976. Those attitudes have influenced many an actor who trained there and account for many of the divisions that we now find in acting circles. Well you can't be a real actor if you don't do the classics? You can't be a real actor if you speak in your own accent, can you?

Aye there's the rub. Us Jocks speak with the wrong accent to be proper actors!

Now I was on the teaching course, so the pressures on me were not the same as on the actors. I witnessed perfectly nice, talented actors get completely screwed up about their Scottish vowel sounds because they thought they would never get into the Royal Shakespeare Company. One friend was even told to stop hanging around with his old pals because it would hinder him losing his accent.

Even at seventeen, I thought that this was appalling. Why should a Scottish actor have to aim for the RSC? Why couldn't he aim for the Traverse or the Lyceum or the Citizens? Was that not good enough? (I found out later that all these theatres were operating on a sort of sub-English rep agenda and that the Cits didn't even audition in Scotland. The attitude was that if you were any good then you would be based in London and have lost the accent.)

I never have had any ambition to work at the National or the RSC but if I say that to actors who have worked there they generally smile smugly and think, "Yes they all say that until the call comes, they just haven't been asked because they aren't good enough." And that may be true, but I do know that even if I was asked I wouldn't want to go. I want to live and work here in Scotland. Of course

I work away and enjoy it, but the prospect of moving to Stratford, leaving my kids and my home, to say ten lines in a Shakespeare has never really appealed to me. But many actors have no choice. I am lucky to have a choice, but even at eighteen I couldn't see what all the fuss was about. I've seen a lot of very bad actors get away with crimes against acting while hiding in a Shakespeare play.

A lot of the snobbery is due to the press and the hype. All the reviewers who supposedly matter live and work in London where the vast majority of theatre, film and television is made. A reviewer goes out, spots someone in a play, tells the world that they are wonderful, they start getting lots of press, directors who live in London go and see them and give them other roles and hey presto they are a star. That does not make them better actors than the actors at the Yorkshire Playhouse or the Lyceum, they are just more visible. We are invisible to that Metropolitan press. It never ceases to amaze me that theatres in Scotland pay more attention to a review in the *Telegraph* or the *Guardian* than a Scottish paper. It seems ludicrous when the vast majority of your audience will be reading *The Scotsman* and they are your paying public. Many a production has trekked around this country playing to three lesbians and a whippet with reviews in the *Independent* and *Sunday Times* to die for. This is all due to the fact that reviewers know nothing about acting anyway, and that these London-based papers know little or nothing about Scottish theatre.

The Traverse only got on the map because these reviewers started to come up for the Festival, and the atmosphere in there made it the place to be for a drink and to meet folk. So, while they were there, they thought that they might as well take in a couple of shows, and nearly died when they discovered that John Byrne could actually write, and that Scots could act pretty brilliantly, even in a Scots accent.

By this I do not mean that actors are only good if they stick with one accent. That would be stupid. Any actor worth their salt has to have the ability to do as many accents as possible and to do them well. If actors want to get on then they need to be as good as they can be. And get noticed. The only way to do that in the seventies was to move south.

The problem for many who went south was that they not only had to be able to act but also had to become different people. That is so hard. I remember having this conversation with the wonderful Phyllis Logan who is not only a great actress but has a fabulous gift for accents. She told me that she found going in and doing auditions in other accents no problem—the difficulty was in being herself. But it was really hard to tell a gag or have a laugh in a different accent because your whole personality is rooted in another culture.

So there we all were, wandering around Draaamaa Scoool, with the weirdest bastardisations of accents you ever heard. A mixture of bad Received Pronunciation, Scots and very unusual grammar. A group of us were once asked by a fellow student in a bad Noel Coward accent "Are youse ones going for the bus?" This guy was from Paisley!

*   *   *   *

After a few months of watching them go through all they had to, I thought no, that is not for me. I couldn't do that. I did not want to be an actor. I wanted to be a singer. A pop star. I could never say that, but I was writing a lot of my own songs and singing *à la* Joni Mitchell and Carol King. I became known as the chanter of my year.

It happened like this . . .

Every year there was a student cabaret. The third-years and the staff were the invited audience, the second-years provided the food, drink, decorated the hall and ran the disco, and the first-years had to provide an hour's cabaret. Auditions were held and, under pressure from my pals, I reluctantly put my name down. The theme was the sixties and I didn't know what to do. So I went in and said that

I would dress up as a flower child and sing at the piano. I sang 'Our House' by Crosby, Stills, Nash and Young and I got the gig. I wasn't the main attraction—in fact I was put on as a filler to cover a scene change for the finale. It's often the way that people ignore what is under their nose, a recurrent theme in my career. If you do not stomp around having tantrums and crises then people ignore you. So the reaction to me was a shock to everyone involved.

On the night I wore a kaftan, flowers and butterflies in my hair, sat down at the piano and sang. When I finished the crowd went bananas. They were screaming and clapping. I walked off, totally numb but they wouldn't stop. I had to do an encore, which of course I hadn't prepared, so I went back on and sang one of my own. They liked that too. It was amazing and wonderful and I was overwhelmed. I became known as "the singer", so that is what I wanted to be. . . .

At the end of my first year I felt that I had got somewhere and knew that it was time to spread my wings further. I got a flat in the West End of Glasgow with my friends Susan and the mad Pam. I got a summer job, broke up with my boyfriend of two years, who found the threat of this former schoolgirl from Newarthill becoming a singer, living in her own flat and being at drama school all too much. I was broken hearted, even though I knew it could never work.

Above:
Jocky Wilson, 1959.

Left:
Aged 3, 1961.
I've always known how to give that 'just staring past the camera at something more interesting' look! Great kilt, eh?

Opposite:
Mum and Dad,
Blackpool.

Right:
Mum in 1970s frock, with
family friend Jim. In 1970
I thought that the Coltness
Hotel and chicken in a basket
were the most sophisticated
things in the world.

Below left:
1972—I told my mother
to burn this photograph!
14 with raging hormones—
I thought I was gorgeous
and so ugly all at the same
time—much the same as I
do now!

Below right:
1974—a 'prefect'
and good girl.

Above: Aunt Margaret, Aunt Joan and Mum. 'The posh aunties'. Not really—but Mum's side of the family were educated, and lived in bought houses. Very elegant and a huge influence on me. I love hats like that.

Below: Papa—Winston Churchill lookalike and a very funny man.

Below: Uncle Andy (Dad's wee brother and Gene Kelly lookalike), Dad (Jimmy), Aunt Frances and Mum (Stella).

Above:
Motherwell Trades and Labour, 1973.

Right:
First ever folk band—
Mark, me and Billy. We
thought we were
'Crosby, Stills and
Nash'. We were actually
more like Glens,
Hutchison and Stepek!

Above: My cousin Kate. Great singer.

Opposite: The wee singer with the band—
complete with 1976 velvet jumpsuit. Gorgeous. . . .

Left:
Drama school, 1975.
Terrified but trying
not to look like
Motherwell.

Below:
Nessie (Gwen's mum),
me (Farrah Fawcett
flicks!), Gwen (my
best friend and future
bridesmaid) and Stella
(great hairdo).
My mother didn't like
our pink hoods with
our gowns, and said
that we should have
worn the white hoods
as the photos would
be nicer! I explained
that I would have had
to do a different
degree for a white
hood, but it made no
difference. . . .

Above: Caterpillar dispute. Me very serious, but politics is a serious business! On the left are John Brannan (an uncle!) and Campbell Christie, and on the far right is the great Mick McGahey.

Below: Elsie Tanner! (I was supposed to be Cinderella!)

Below: Hunners of badges!

Left:
When you start in the business you think you have to look like this! The photographer was a more than seedy character, too!! When Philip Differ saw this at the Comedy Unit, he said he thought they were getting some sexy chic—unfortunately I walked in and ruined it all!

Below:
Gold in his Boots, 1982.
Jonathan Watson, and me
as Kate.
7:84.

Above:
At the Pleasance in 1982.
My first 'mammie' role,
with Myra McFadyen.
Brand New Wildcats.

Right:
First Dame.
Cinderella, 1983.
Borderline.

Above: The original *Naked Video* team, 1985.

Below: The fabulous *Nippy Sweeties* . . .
(Angie Rew was the other member, but not in this photo). The wonderful
Liz Lochhead is on the right. I was constipated!!

Above:
'Knackered'.
With Katie, aged
3 months, in 1988.

Right:
'Hey, Calam!'

Above:
The original cast of
The Steamie, 1987—
Kate Murphy,
Ida Schuster, me
and Dorothy Paul
(tenement goddess).

Opposite:
Dignity,
always dignity.

Right:
Delia Smith.
Mary's favourite
recipe—take 50p, buy
chips, eat them. . . .

Next page:
Faith, Hope . . .
Calamity.
Little did they know
when they set out on
this journey, circa
1970, where it would
all end. . . .

So a new life started. I ate my first take-away curries, stayed out all night, drank too much, smoked dope, hung around with gay men and women, sung in dives with various bands and generally had a ball. I shopped at Goodies at one in the morning, went to millions of parties and bought my clothes at Laura Ashley. My sister Louise reminded me the other day how she and her friends used to taunt me as I flounced past in my floor length white smock dress with matching pinafore in blue. I thought that I was gorgeous, they thought that I was a total weirdo. They used to shout obscenities at me when I stood at the bus stop (it's a quaint Lanarkshire custom—anything different, they shout obscenities or throw things). The Bellshill branch of Laura Ashley hadn't opened yet!

I loved the Bohemian life. The first time I headed into Laura I thought I was so grown up. It had just opened at the top of Byres Road and I had never really been at that end of the street before, I'd only really got to the underground and back. So, when I ventured up that end, fighting my way through the throng of Pre-Raphaelite students in love beads and patchouli oil, I couldn't believe what I saw. The road seemed to open up and the Grosvenor Hotel looked like the most glamourous and elegant thing that I had ever seen—it seemed to go on for miles. I could see the BBC, the Botanic Garden—I didn't know they existed. The whole place was like I imagined London or

New York to be. Living there was great, and I could imagine that I was as bright and sophisticated as I thought everyone else was.

*   *   *   *

After two years of the high life, I couldn't get away from Glasgow fast enough. I was bored with college, bored with singing and working in the same places without getting noticed—no record company ever spotted us— and by now a lot of the people on the course had outgrown each other. I hung on to get my Diploma by the skin of my teeth, although I was not a particularly good student latterly. I was singing and making money, but my university dissertation was late (part of the teaching course was done at Glasgow University and if you did not pass that you did not graduate), and I sort of disintegrated during the last six months. Another long term relationship had bitten the dust very painfully, and I was heavily involved in student politics. The then Labour government had just brought in massive education cuts and our postgraduate courses were cut, which meant that some of us could not finish our qualification. So we marched into the Director of the Academy's office, asked him to leave and we stayed there for two days! Then we marched up to Jordanhill and did the same. Occupations like these in universities and colleges spawned a new political generation—if you look at politicians of all parties now in their 40s, you can guarantee that many of them were involved in the education campaign in the 1970s. This was certainly the real stimulus for my politics. I had always been interested and came from a staunch Labour background, but actually participating and trying to change something for the better was a wonderful experience.

You can see why I was finding the boring old life of exams and college less than exciting. All the good stuff seemed to be outside in the real world and I desperately wanted to be a part of it. Even comedy was learnt not by doing shows in the college or in class but in the canteen. I wasn't funny at college but I learned fast. I was too young and naive to be quick-witted, and I usually found myself either the butt of jokes or the feed. The funny people were John Wood and Annette Staines—they were hilarious and we all felt that they would go on to become top turns. We were a sort of threesome and I loved just being a part of all the gags. I also learned the value of staying quiet and then coming out with a surprise funny line. That taught me timing, I'll tell you. Jonathan Watson was another regular in this group, usually when we were pished in the Ivanhoe Hotel next door. He has been a great pal for years, even though he always confessed that he fancied me after he had six pints. I would have taken it as a compliment had he not been saying it to every other woman in the room! Great laughs though . . . and we did all the usual daft gags—getting the janny to read out messages over the tannoy system was a favourite. "Would Hugh Jarse please come to the main foyer, Hugh Jarse."

Actually when I think back on it all now, I don't know how I graduated at all. My biggest fault is that I take on too much, thinking that without me the world will collapse, when the world will carry on quite happily and successfully without me.

So, I survived drama school. But I didn't excel—partly my fault, partly the course. I left feeling even more confused about who I was, where I was going and where I had come from. Any talent that I thought I had when I arrived had been devalued—even my singing. I was totally insecure and I wanted to run away and start afresh.

What was valued by the college was not what I valued. Success for them was turning out another conveyor belt actor with a bland RP accent who would fight it out in London along with the hundreds of other similarly bland actors who were looking for work. Individuality was not encouraged. I felt vindicated when I read that Tom Courtenay had refused to change his accent when at drama school, as did the wonderful Sandy Morton. I'm sure that's one of the reasons why they are such good actors. But things like singing or comedy were not deemed as important. Real actors were people who did dramatic roles. It's the same now. When was the last time you saw a comedy actor win an Oscar? Yet they are usually the people that the audience queue up to see.

The chip on my shoulder was growing into a fish supper. It wasn't a bitter chip, just one that told me that I wasn't good enough even to try acting and that I should get back in my box pretty smart. And that's exactly what I did. I gave up the band, the flat, the dreams and accepted a place at teacher training college. Where? Well, where does any Glaswegian go when they want to start again? EDINBURGH. . . .

8

CLUBLAND

During drama school I had started singing professionally.
I made a lot of money and gained loads of experience. The
band that I was with were a great bunch and very talented,
but the work was soul destroying. If you were insecure
before you started it only got worse. I have total admiration
for the acts that work so hard in clubs because it really is
the toughest audience in the world, mainly because, once
they employ you, they think that you are their property.
Which means that they can talk right through you as you
work your butt off, and that they have the right to say
anything they want. You are just a turn, "so don't come

any of your airs and graces. In here, you'll get changed in the lavvy the same as everyone else!"

*　　*　　*　　*

Clubs. Those hotbeds of liberalism, tolerance and politically correct, non-sexist behaviour. I'm not just talking about working-men's, miners' welfare and all that, I'm talking about golf clubs and bowling clubs as well.

What is it with private clubs? They are supposed to be set up for people's enjoyment but they have got more rules than anything else. You would think that when you entered a club there would be a big sign saying:

COME IN AND WELCOME.
HOPE YOU ALL ENJOY YOURSELVES
AND THE HOSPITALITY OF THE CLUB.
ENJOY THE CHEAP DRINK,
THE COMPANY AND HASTE YE BACK!

No way! The signs always say things like:

NO CARDIGANS IN THE MAIN LOUNGE.

NO STOVIES TO BE EATEN DURING THE TURNS.

NO BREATHING DURING THE BINGO.

NO LAUGHING DURING THE CABARET.

NO CHILDREN TO BE FOUND ON THE PREMISES
BETWEEN THE HOURS OF 8AM TO 7AM. ANY
THAT ARE WILL BE TAKEN OUTSIDE AND TIED TO A
LAMPPOST AND FORCED TO WATCH 3 BOWLING TIES.

NO WOMEN ALLOWED IN WITHOUT A MAN.

NO CATHOLICS EVER.

NO JEWS, NO BLACKS, NOBODY BUT US!

US . . . WEE BALDY, NIPPED-IN, MASONIC GITS WITH
TERYLENE TROUSERS PULLED UP TO THEIR NECKS.

Those clubs don't allow women to be on the board, or
to vote, or to even play bowls on any day that isn't a
"Ladies Day". Of course, the boys can come out and chuck
their balls any time that they want. But, if a woman is
spotted hovering any distance away from the tea urn on
a man's day, then they're practically out with the sniper
rifles!

They operate in a climate of fear and any woman that
is brave enough to ask questions or to want things to be
equal is ostracised and branded a troublemaker. The other
women, usually wives of the committee, are too afraid of

what may happen at home if they agree with them. So they do their best to allow their husbands to save face, and in turn ostracise the said troublemakers. This may not seem a big deal, but when your friends and social life revolve around a club, taking on a set of rules, regardless of how unjust, can have a devastating effect on a woman's life. I'm glad to say that a few brave women have made a stand in the face of very tough opposition and have started to win through.

But it's not only bowling clubs or miners' welfares. There are golf clubs—full of guys with second names as first names and who all talk a bit like Chic Murray, though nowhere near as funny—well not intentionally anyway.

"What's that yer saying Cameron? You are kidding Farquhar? A wumman in the main lounge? Dear God what's the world coming to! And whit? She's wearing trousers? Wait till I tell Blair about this!"

Years ago I was working with my band in one of those golf clubs, I won't say where—Newton Mearns—and I found myself with some time to spare after the band had set up so I wandered into the main lounge. It was a lovely lounge with a big main window almost like a conservatory that looked out over the 18th hole. It was all plush carpet and parquet flooring in the window area. I decided to go and watch the guys teeing off. As I stood by the window I felt a tap on my shoulder. As I looked around, I heard a guy saying "I'm sorry madam but ladies are not allowed to step off the carpet." Eh? What did he think I was going to do? Leak oestrogen all over the parquet floor?

The religious divide is the worst, though, and the West of Scotland has a lot to answer for, and they're all as bad as each other. I spent many a night in Orange clubs and Hibs clubs all over the West of Scotland and I view it as a profound learning experience. All the guys whether Catholic or Protestant, had to change their names to suit each club we performed in. Well you couldn't play an Orange club with a name like Kevin Barry or a Knights club with a name like Mason Boyne!

But all these clubs have one thing in common—the compère. What is it with these guys? They swagger a lot and point at innocent women in the audience, and although they are plumbers or joiners during the week, on a Saturday night down the club they turn into a combination of Tony Bennett and Sammy Davis Jr! They start talking in this sorta mid-Atlantic accent, usually out of the side of their mouths, and stun people with their wit and ability to talk pish for minutes at a time!

In one particular Orange club the compère was a complete one-off. His outfit was topped off by the thing he wore on his head. He had obviously had a brainstorm while walking past a pet shop and thought "Hey, there's a hamster. I think I'll buy that and pop it on my napper!

And even though it's a completely different colour from the rest of my hair, nobody will notice, will they?" So he swans around, wondering why people are having conversations with his forehead unable to keep their eyes off the thing that has attached itself to his head.

On one occasion he came into the dressing room to talk to us. Now I was only around seventeen or eighteen and there I was in my velvet jumpsuit (well it was the seventies) and I thought I was lovely. I had been given a gift by a friend of a small, plain silver cross and was wearing it that night. The compère was chatting away when he suddenly burst into a fit of "ho, hey, ho, ho. Whit's that roon your neck hen?" And pointed to the cross.

I said "Oh, it's just a cross, my pal gave it to me."

"Oh naw hen, ye cannie wear that in here," he says.

"But its okay, it's just a plain Church of Scotland cross, see," I said holding it up.

"Oh, it's no me hen but ye cannie wear that in here. If wan of they bastards oot there in the audience thinks ther's a wee man on that they'll haul you off the stage with it"!

A wee man on it . . . dear God! . . . and I had to take it off.

*   *   *   *

A song written by my dear friend Dave Anderson completely sums up for me all those days in the clubs. We had some great laughs but it was hard bloody work, when the bingo gets better order than the band. . . .

WAN SINGER, WAN SONG

Youse all know me I'm Harry McDade,
Through the week I'm a plumber to trade,
But come the weekend, I've got it made,
I'm a singer.

Youse are here for the crack and the booze,
We havnae got any Darkies or Jews,
And youse'll get barred if any of youse
Goes yer dinger.

Wan singer, Wan song,
No children, no denims,
No dancing, no swearing,
Wan singer, wan song.

Efter all the work yous've done,
You deserve a wee bit of fun,
But we'll have none of last weeks carry on,
Yon was murder.

Youse are here for to set yourself free,
That's the game, that's okay by me,
But if yez don't mind, we'll just have a wee
Bit of order.

Wan singer, wan song,
No politics, no religion,
No Catholics, no poofters,
Wan singer, wan song.

We've got music and we've got booze,
We've got cabaret, and we've got booze,
We've got bingo and we've got booze
At the Welfare.

Wan singer, wan song,
No freedom, no progress,
No nothin, no danger,
Wan singer wan song. . . .

*   *   *   *

Two incidents made me decide to get out of clubs and
almost made me give up singing for good.

The first was a conversation I had with my drummer,
Ronnie Leckie. He was a fab drummer who must have

been in his thirties. One of those guys that should have been on tour with Elton John because he was good enough, but like so many really good musos, just didn't get the breaks at the right time and ended up with commitments and a full-time job. But he knew the business. He hadn't been that keen on me when I started. I was just another girl singer with a good voice, but not a great voice. I had none of the pyrotechnics that they love in clubs. I didn't yodel like Patsy Cline or go for big notes like Shirley Bassey, but I did my best. It was a style of singing that I had never really done before and I found it difficult. Someone whose idol was Joni Mitchell was never really going to find a sympathetic audience in Larkhall Miners' Welfare.

Anyway, I arrived early at a gig and found myself tinkering at the piano and doing some of my own songs. I didn't see Ronnie come in and he sat and listened. When I finished he got up and walked across and said, "Elaine don't get stuck here. You have to get out and do what you can with that talent. If you don't take a risk now then you will end up just another club act. I didn't know you could sing like that. Go and do it before its too late," and he walked away. I was overwhelmed. But I knew he was right. I was going for the easy option and it was killing me.

That conversation planted a seed and I began to think

that I should leave. A similar discussion with Andy Cameron shortly afterwards convinced me that I should go. He was so kind and encouraging and I will never forget that.

The second incident was the final straw. It confirmed all my fears and insecurities. It was my last gig and we were in East Kilbride Rolls Royce Club. As the band were setting up I went to the bar and bought a round of drinks. When I came back I did something that I had never done before. Everyone in bands knows that you never sit drinks anywhere near the electrical equipment. I stupidly sat a pint on top of the piano player's expensive new keyboard and it fell over into the piano rendering it useless. I was mortified. I apologised for about an hour, as Iain tried to fix it, without success, before giving up and resorting to using the old club organ.

It was a nightmare. I couldn't stop crying, so by the time I went onstage I was a wreck. I was too much of an amateur to put it behind me. And so I learned another valuable lesson: when you feel like shit, don't let the audience see it—it ain't what they pay for. But I didn't know it then. I sang through a veil of tears and didn't hit many good notes. This was topped off by a very drunk woman walking up to me and saying "See you hen, you're the effin worst singer I've ever heard in my effin life." That was it. I left showbiz for good. . . .

I graduated from the RSAMD, making my parents happy and headed for teacher training. I was nineteen.

THE PRIME OF
MISS ELAINE SMITH

I turned my back on my dreams and all the nonsense that filled my head and determined to make a new life in Edinburgh. I was doing my teacher training, I would be a good teacher, get a good job, get married and live what I regarded as a safe life. I got a place at Moray House College and a room in the halls of residence.

I had spent the summer in London and loved it. I had turned twenty and was at just the right time in my life to be in London on my own. I went to the theatre, cinemas, restaurants, galleries and discovered a resilience that I did not know I had. That time in London gave me back a love of theatre that drama school had almost destroyed. I saw *Evita* and *Chorus Line*. I got a bit of perspective back. I went everywhere on my own and I loved being in a city that didn't bat an eyelid at a young woman in a restaurant alone. I came home a more mature person, worked in the local hotel and stayed with my parents. I really enjoyed that and felt ready to embark on a teaching career. Now I wanted to be a member of the audience, no longer the star of the show.

On my first day at college, one of my lecturers, Gareth Wardell, said, "Are you sure this is what you want to do?" I said "Oh yes." Then he said "It just appears to me that you would be ideal for a company like 7:84 or Wildcat." I couldn't believe it. I had spent three years at drama school and not one lecturer had ever spoken to me like that, never mind seen any potential. I just laughed it off saying that chance would be a fine thing.

Anyway, I had other things to prove to myself and they were mainly about my ability to work hard and learn. By this time I realised just how much of my education I had squandered. I really wished that I had been more diligent and basically learnt more. I envied those students who had been in their 20s and 30s at college because they got so much more out of the course. I was just too young. I had a lot of catching up to do.

So I worked really hard and did well. I passed all my exams and teaching practices, even got an A in Psychology and got some confidence back. I felt that I had at last found something that I was good at.

I did a teaching practice with a woman who became a dear friend and still is. Pam Wardell was the finest teacher I had ever met. Her passion and commitment to children was astounding and from the first day I walked into Firrhill High I felt as if I was coming home. I loved it, and when I got a job there as soon as I left Moray House I felt I was so lucky.

Teaching was possibly the hardest job that I have ever done. I used to come home and sit down about four thirty and before I knew it it would be seven o'clock. For about a month I couldn't arrange to do anything because I was in a permanent state of collapse. I would wake up at seven with none of the lights on and not know where I was, focus, get up and make my tea, have a bath and go to bed. Knackered. That's why teachers look so bad. You are on your feet six hours a day, engaged in a never-ending struggle to keep your second-year mental cases under some sort of control.

I was only 22 when I started and uniform was not compulsory, so 5th and 6th year pupils didn't look that much different from me. I was in my New Romantic phase, and would turn up at school in my black flying suit with hunners of zips, thigh length boots, and a leather jacket. The hierarchy thought I was mad, but put it down to the fact that I was from the West and taught drama. Nuff said. . . .

Once, I even found myself getting a bollocking from another member of staff who didn't realise that I was a teacher. I was using the school hall for a drama about a flood and the kids had to climb up onto the roofs to get away from the flooding and be rescued. So there we all were, standing on the tables in the hall shouting for help, when this teacher walked in and bawled at us. She was screaming at us to stop this nonsense and what did we think we were doing, when I walked forward and introduced myself. She left very sheepishly, which the kids loved. She never asked what we were actually doing, but not many did ask about drama. If they taught English, they thought they knew what we did, and if they didn't they were too afraid to ask.

There is a sort of gallows humour that exists amongst teachers and some of the funniest and weirdest people I have ever met are in that profession. After a few years it turns everyone a bit mad. I started out determined that I would never sound like any of my old teachers, but about six months into the job, I found myself shouting "Walk on the left, now!" You start to understand why routine becomes so important to staff. Why they use the same cups, sit in the same seats, play bridge or do the *Guardian* crossword with the same people. It's because, outside those staff-room doors, it's a zoo over which you have very little control, so you control the wee bits that you can. I knew it was time to leave when I was looking forward to my coffee in the staff room more than teaching a class. It's a kind of siege mentality.

One teacher I know had a great device for keeping the mental kids in check. He had a walk-in cupboard at the back of his class and used to have his fags and coffee in there for a wee break. He would set the class some work and to stop them getting too rowdy he would attach a plastic eye, about a foot long, to the top of the blackboard to keep watch. He would tell the class that the eye was watching and would transmit any misbehaviour to him. Of course, as soon as he went into the cupboard the noise would start, but what the kids didn't realise was that he could hear their voices. So they were amazed that when the teacher came back, he always knew exactly who had been talking. He would go through a big charade with the eye, asking who had misbehaved and the eye would "tell" him. "Right McNulty, out here. . . ." the kids would be astonished. It never failed, the eye got them every time! Ingenuity, a teacher's best friend.

*　　*　　*　　*

I had three of the most fulfilling years of my life there, but by the time I left, things had changed within me. I was only 23 and still had so much to learn myself. I have always believed that the best teachers are those with experience of life and after three years all my life experience had run out. I needed to go and live some more myself. I had a feeling that things were going to change and I felt myself being propelled towards making other life choices but did not really know what to do.

Many things brought me to the path that I was about to take.

The first was politics. I had always been very interested in politics. So, I again joined the Students' Representative Council, this time at Moray House. I wasn't that fired up but wanted to carry on my political involvement. When I became a teacher I joined the EIS and that was it really. I became a teacher just as the Clegg report and various cuts in education were coming into place. There were many strikes and marches and I was involved in every one—not because I was some great political activist but because I felt that the cuts in education were totally wrong and that an already underfunded service was being run into the ground. None of the powers-that-be really cared about the comprehensive system because their kids were all at fee-paying schools. As usual, the state system was good enough for other people's kids but not for theirs. That sort of attitude was so prevalent in Edinburgh that I found it quite staggering, and still do.

I also got very involved with the women's movement. I read lots of books like *The Women's Room* and *Beyond the Fragments* and started to get angry, asking questions that no one could answer. Why were there only about two female headteachers of secondary schools in the whole of Scotland? Why did I have to be a wife and mother? Why did I have to live the same life that my mother had? I started to question everything about my life. About the way I dressed, the way men spoke to me, the way it was expected that I would marry and give up my career. Why? I was fulfilled by my job as much as any relationship and didn't see why I had to give anything up. As I began to ask these questions so did many other women, and I found huge comfort, friendship and support from the women I met through Women's Voice and Women's Fightback.

I don't want to sound like a bad Fay Weldon novel, but these women were great. We had great laughs. I met my dear pal Chris around this time and we were sort of soulmates because we were politically active but working-class. Most of the women were from quite posh backgrounds and were a wee bit in awe of us because we were real punters. They didn't know what to make of us and Chris used to love watching them try to cope with me because I would be dead active and committed but I still wore all my make-up, had long hair and wore jumpsuits and thigh-length boots! You have to understand that the thought police were around in the women's movement and if you didn't wear the correct uniform—i.e. no make-up, double-woman sign earrings, cropped hair, denims and hunners of badges—then there would be talk. Eventually I did modify my style and cut my hair, got hunners of badges and a denim jacket but I still went for the diamanté earrings! Chris still winds me up about all that. She was a breath of fresh air in the p.c. world of the eighties and we also shared a great love of football—the Sellick, of course.

I became that feminist wumman selling papers outside the St James Centre. There was always a great emphasis on selling the paper. I don't know why. Maybe they wanted to bore women to death, because it certainly wouldn't motivate them. They didn't have to see the word STRUGGLE written 2000 times. Most of them were struggling on an hourly basis. I used to diligently read my copy, then go and buy a *Cosmopolitan*. But somehow or other I did sell quite a lot of papers. I think it was because I had a working-class accent and I smiled a lot. I also left the donkey jacket at home. My innate sense of fashion never let me stoop that low although I did have a Palestinian scarf. I couldn't believe how dowdy the

Edinburgh Left were. Generally, Edinburgh fashion is of a more muted and conservative nature than Glasgow fashion, which was always more in your face. If I arrived back in Edinburgh from a weekend in Glasgow, I immediately felt overdressed. Come to think of it I spent three years feeling overdressed! It was the New Romantic phase, but there weren't many dandy highwaymen cutting about the Royal Mile. . . .

Anyway, my social life started to revolve around my politics. Whether it was Women's Fightback, Rank and File Teachers, the Anti Nazi League, Nicaraguan Solidarity, El Salvador, the Socialist Workers Party socials or Vegans for Dolphins, I was there.

It finally hit me that there had to be more to life than this when I found myself sitting at an SWP tea. In a posh house in Marchmont, there we sat with tea and scones and talked about Revolution. It was time to move on. I wanted to be in politics but the far Left seemed more interested in fund raising than in actually doing anything that would benefit those in need living in dire poverty only a couple of miles away. If the answer to every question is Revolution then it lets you off the hook from actually doing anything. You can just sit back, secure in your theory and dogma, criticising everyone else. It didn't escape my notice that most of the people involved were professionals with a salary probably three times what my father earned, living in lovely bought houses in nice areas. Nobody was living in Pilton. I didn't doubt their sincerity, just the methodology. It was all theory. I knew that the working class would never listen to them—(1) because they would immediately be identified as posh because of their accents and (2) because of their clothes. It was a well-known fact that during the sixties when the Marxists tried to go into places like Harlem and recruit, none of the dudes would listen to them because they dressed so badly. Che Guevara fashion hadn't hit the Bronx. That's why Tommy Sheridan has such popularity and respect among working people. He looks good, dresses sharp and although he is dead brainy and went to university, he talks like one of us.

The Left argued all the time and no one ever got it right. I had this vision that if the Revolution was happening in Corstorphine the Lefties would all be sitting in Mathers Bar arguing about what bus to get, while the punters got on with the fighting.

My dear pal Elaine Collins told me a great story that summed up the far Left for me. She was coming out of a tube station in London to find all the Leftie paper sellers lined up as they always are on a Friday. It was the week that Nelson Mandela was released from prison but the headlines that greeted Elaine were things like *Mandela— A Sell-Out?* The rest of the world rejoiced while the Left were asking if Mandela had sold out! Can you only be a real hero if you die in prison?

But it all gave me a great grounding in politics.

Although I had gone to Edinburgh to forget all dreams of performing, within months I found myself being drawn in that direction once more and I decided to go and audition for Edinburgh University Theatre Co. Here, I could start afresh, without all the baggage of drama school. To my surprise I was offered a great part in a great play, David Mamet's *Sexual Perversity in Chicago*. I had to play an American, Joan, and it was brilliant. I discovered how much I really loved acting, and I spent the next couple of years doing different plays on an amateur level—all of which went well and got good reviews. One particularly memorable review came from Joyce McMillan in the *Guardian*. The play was Ben Jonson's *Bartholomew Fair* and I played Ursula the pig woman (with Alan Little, now the BBC's Africa correspondent, as my sidekick Mooncalf— he reminded me of this at Kirsty Wark's wedding some years ago!). Anyway, Joyce wrote a very good review that stated that I would not be out of place in any Glasgow Fish Market. She obviously saw Mary Nesbitt in me long before I did!

So acting and singing were firmly back on the agenda. But I was very, very sad to leave teaching. I felt I had done a good job. Although I was far from perfect, I had worked hard and cared. I still see some of the pupils who write to me or come and see shows that I am in. They are all married with three kids now, but still call me Miss when I bump into them on Princes Street. I really missed the kids and the staff room, and all the girls in the office who put up with me—especially Christine, who had that great, droll Edinburgh sense of humour. I had some of the best laughs of my life in that staff room with Ed Cooper, Alan Hunter, Dave Clark and the unforgettable AJ Savage—a comic genius of the Eric Morecambe school. These men taught me how to deal with everything from severe slagging and provocation, to political debates. And they also gave me a desire to move to a job where I didn't have to endure the *Guardian* crossword every day. Ironically, actors turned out to be worse crossword fiends than the teachers ever were.

With all this experience there was only one place to go really. 7:84 and Wildcat.

10

ANOTHER OPENING . . .

At the top of Leith Walk after a night at the Reggae Club, the man who is now my husband and I had a humdinger of a fight. Okay, a few swallies or tinctures had been taken, but it wasn't your usual "domestic". Bob basically started giving me a lecture (he's good at that!) about what I was doing with my life. He said that I was throwing any talent that I had away and that he didn't want to know me in ten years time when I was standing in a pub saying "Well I could have been an actor or a singer but I was too scared." I tried to deny all this but I knew it was true. It didn't stop me stomping off up the road on my todd. I was furious. How dare he say that to me even if it was true. But I had to face the fact that I was scared. Terrified of the risk. I had done it before and it had all gone wrong and I did not want to feel like that again.

His words nagged away at me and so I sat down and wrote to Wildcat, the company that I had always wanted to work with. May as well aim high. . . .

My love affair with 7:84 and Wildcat had really started when I was at drama school. The only "play" I ever remember seeing before college was on TV. It was called *The Cheviot, the Stag and the Black, Black Oil.* I don't remember very much about it now, but I do remember feeling captivated by it and that previously I had never wanted to watch a play all the way through. I didn't even know who wrote it, but it had music and song and really good actors, and it stuck in my memory.

At college someone said that they were going to the Cits to see 7:84. I didn't know what that was. They explained and mentioned *The Cheviot*, saying that I would like it because they were political and they had a great band. That'll do for me, I thought. When I watched that show, *Out of our Heads*, I knew at long last what I wanted to do. I really did want to stand up in the audience and shout "I can do that." I felt like I belonged, and that for the first time in a theatre, here were a group of actors speaking directly to me. When Terry Neason started to sing one of Dave Anderson's songs that was it. I was blown away. Terry was my new hero, replacing Barbra Streisand forever!

It is easy for the pundits and the Arts Council to dismiss this kind of theatre, as we sit here in the late nineties. But it was a very different story in the late seventies. Agitprop (agitation and propaganda) brought a whole new audience into the theatre, and, by incorporating sketches, music and dance with the burning issues of the day, they allowed people to hang on to the Variety skills that were on the wane. I was thinking that the other night at *The Celtic Story* when I watched Jimmy Logan employ all his magical skills as a song and dance man, a comedian and an actor, to bring great life to an agitprop show. It seemed like things had come full circle.

The impact of 7:84 was huge in the West of Scotland due to the large working-class population who were being ignored by many theatres which were putting on sub-RSC/National seasons for the middle-classes or bad Variety shows which were well past their sell-by date.

At their best 7:84 and Wildcat were magnificent, incorporating music, comedy, politics, and social issues—all delivered with as much of a working-class accent as some of the middle-class actors and actresses could muster.

At present that type of theatre is viewed as a tired form, but I predict its return—when it gets an injection of youth that will make it their own, a lot of cash, and those two essentials: good writing and good performing.

But in 1977 it was wonderful.

Ever since then I'd wanted to work with one of these companies, but had always felt deep down that it was a pipe dream. I'd even done my thesis at university on them, but got completely tongue-tied when I had to go and interview them. It is strange looking back now, having known the two great men, Dave Anderson and Dave MacLennan for sixteen years, that I could ever have been so in awe of them.

So, after my fight with Bob, I went home and wrote to them. I had also written to a company in London, called Broadside Mobile Workers Theatre. This was when I was at my most political and I thought they sounded ideal for me. So I went down and auditioned. It was awful. They were a classic far Left organisation with great earnest intentions of changing the world, but the stuff they were doing was terminally boring. Ibsen for the workers, but without the laughs and slapstick! Why would you want to lecture people about how bad their lives are during their lunchtime? They fucking know already—they are the ones who are living it! That patronising attitude makes me crazy, but at the time I just felt intimidated and thought that they were right. Boring, but right.

As is often the case, they were mainly upper-class, public

school types, fuelled by guilt about the wealth and status of their parents, but with the luxury of a cushion of money to supplement their profit-share boring of the working-classes. There was a uniform, which usually consisted of little washing and wearing the dowdiest clothes ever. There was also a terror of not addressing people correctly for fear of causing offence, particularly to women. So they called each other comrade—but assured you that this had nothing to do with communist party hijacking of the word. They were Trotskyist and used it to create a non-sexist environment. Great eh? They also used sister or brother, which could be said with amazing rage, giving me a glimpse of the tension and anger that existed behind their facade of comradeship.

I wanted to laugh but was too scared—particularly of the women, who were all called Petra. They all had the standard issue double-woman sign earrings, no make-up, baggy jumpsuits, and combat boots. I wore a frock and felt like a hooker and a failure, as I had obviously bought into the capitalist machine that crushed women by forcing them to wear lipstick. I would have felt more at home at a Moonies convention.

They toured around doing shows in canteens and workplaces—God only knows what the workers thought. Humour and lightness of touch were clearly not their strong points. But I had to go through with the audition since I had travelled all the way to London. It lasted a day, and not only did I have to act and sing, I had to be grilled on my politics for hours. All that was missing was the rubber truncheon and a light shining in my face! I got the job but was saved at the last minute by the fact that I didn't have an Equity card. Somebody up there likes me.

I expected the same type of thing from an interview with Wildcat or 7:84. And so I was more than a little apprehensive when, two days after I wrote, I got a phone call from Wildcat asking me to come and meet Dave MacLennan in the Cafe Royal for a chat. I was a nervous wreck, but he was lovely. He was like a normal person— well normal for someone in theatre. He said at the end that I seemed an ideal person for Wildcat (I don't know why because he had never seen me act or sing). I think he just took to me. He explained that they were casting later and would get me in for an audition. I floated home. A few weeks later they called and said that they were auditioning. They explained that they were looking for a guy to replace the fabulous Dave Hicks who had been taken ill, but that they felt it would be a good time to see me as they were casting a big show for the Festival starting in July. So off I went.

I was so nervous—though Dave Anderson later confessed that he thought that I was the most confident and macho woman he'd ever met. If only he knew. I was shitting myself!

The band were all very nice and laid back though I do remember Mike Travis smiling at me and making me feel better. Thankfully Terry Neason was not there. I would never have been able to sing in front of her. They were all quite distant and I later found out that it was because they didn't trust MacLennan, since he had said that I was great, then they discovered that he had never seen me act or heard me sing. Even if he had he wouldn't have known because he couldn't sing a note. Fair enough. At the time I just thought they hated me.

Anyway, I sat down at the piano and started to sing a Joni Mitchell number and within a minute they all started to look at me and listen. When I finished they clapped and then Anderson got me to sing scales and then I sat down and did my old standard when I am drunk: 'Leavin on a Jet Plane' and the band joined in.

After that, I think they liked me. They joked and laughed and that was it. I knew there was no job for me but I had done alright and at least they liked me. I left and that was that.

About a week later I got a call in the middle of a class to go to the office. There was a phone call for me. It was John McGrath, another hero of mine and I started to shake as he asked me to come and audition for a part in the new

7:84 Clydebuilt season. He said I had been recommended by Dave MacLennan from their sister company Wildcat. I couldn't believe it. I arranged an interview for after school and I went in to read. I wasn't that nervous because I was still in a state of shock. If I didn't get the job then at least I had got to meet John McGrath.

I called back after six to be told that I had the job. They nearly died when I said I didn't have a Union card, but thanks to the skills of Christine Hamilton, their administrator, they managed to do a deal with Equity and I got a card. (I'm sure Christine regrets that now since she has had to deal with me in panto for the last couple of years as my boss. No easy task!) I handed in my notice at school and moved back to Glasgow where I had bought a flat the year before.

I had started to really miss Glasgow and knew that I wanted to move back so when two great pals (Carol and Jamie) were selling their wee flat in Scotstoun, I decided to buy it. I was really broke and they helped me out a great deal with it. I loved that flat, and here was my chance to live in it full time. I was going to be an actress with my favourite company. Wildcat then phoned and offered me their show in the summer. My God—I had two jobs. . . .

Another new life was about to start.

11

NAKED WITH ZOLA BUDD

The full story of the exploits of an innocent abroad in the
world of showbusiness belong in another book, but you
can have a quick swatch at my cv to see what happened.
I had a great time.

During the three years I stayed with Wildcat, I toured
all over Scotland and parts of England, did shows about
everything from the Health Service and the Miners' strike,
to Nicaragua and class division, and I adored it. I thought
that I had died and gone to heaven. All I wanted to do
was keep working and I could have happily stayed in
theatre forever. I didn't think that I would ever get into

television, because in my own mind I wasn't a "real" actor. Other actors got to do TV, but not me.

So it was a huge surprise when I was spotted by Colin Gilbert, the Head of the Comedy Unit at BBC Scotland. He had seen me in a Wildcat show and offered me a part in *Laugh I Nearly Paid My Licence Fee*. It was only a couple of sketches, but it meant I'd be working with the hugely talented Robbie Coltrane, John Sessions and Louise Gold. It was a great experience. Very exciting. People doing your hair and make-up, bringing you cups of tea—and you got paid. Heaven! We did a song (Myra McFadyen and myself) with Robbie, which was called 'The Glasgow Song'. It was based around a character that Robbie had created, a sort of unintelligible Glaswegian (not unlike Nesbitt now that I think about it) and it was filmed all around Glasgow and was very funny. I was the wife, of course. It was fab.

Colin then offered me a job on *Naked Radio*, where I started working with Gregor Fisher, Tony Roper, Ron Bain, Dave McNiven and Johnny Watson.

I went up to meet Colin Gilbert, or God as he became known, for what I thought was an audition. He chatted to me for 10 minutes and then asked if I would like to do it. I said yes, and ten minutes later I was in the Botanics getting my photo taken for the *Radio Times* with the rest of the team.

It was a fabulous time. I was the only woman in the team but they were great. We also had a brilliant team of writers, including the wonderful Philip Differ, Bob Black and Ian Pattison (again, no women of course). We rehearsed for a day and then recorded live in front of an audience in the Tron.

The first rehearsals were terrifying for me. All these guys who I had watched for years were sitting joking and laughing and I felt so out of place. I was 24 and still didn't feel like a real actor, so I was scared. They were really friendly and nice to me but every time I opened my mouth I felt completely duff! Not only did you have to try and be funny, you had to try and do it in other accents too! Now some accents I can do very easily, but others would take a voice coach and a locked room for a month to help me to get them. Just sitting in a room having a sketch thrown at you that you have never seen before and having to get it up to performance standard in a day is hard, but rehearsing it out loud in front of the team was horrendous.

Apparently when I was hired Colin asked our continuity announcer, Ian Aldred (who had been at drama school with me), if he thought I would be good, as he had been told that I could do a variety of accents. Ian's reply was "Oh yes, a variety of Glasgow accents." I've never forgiven him for that!

Anyway, I struggled through, scared stiff—particularly

when I heard Gregor's fabulous accents. His Isle of Lewis had us in hysterics and I realised that the main requirements to do accents, apart from a good ear, are practice and confidence.

Unfortunately, I had neither when I was presented with Zola Budd. I had to do 'Zola's Diary'—a full page monologue starring me as the diminutive South African runner. It was very funny—but for all the wrong reasons. It was probably the worst attempt at a South African accent that I have ever heard. I started off badly and fell away. I travelled through Sydney, Johannesburg, and the East End of London, via Inverness, in my performance live on the radio. It was appalling, but you are always comforted by other actors when you are involved in something awful (like falling off the stage into the orchestra pit). They always tell you that nobody would have noticed. Possibly, but in this case only if they had been stone deaf!

Within the Comedy Unit, Zola Budd is always brought up as my finest moment. Bastards!

Another of my great moments occurred during this time and the relentless slagging by the Comedy Unit has to be seen to be believed. The joy at others' misfortune, particularly actors that you are friends with, is amazing and very funny. Apart from Colin Gilbert—the boss, His Majesty—who has a wicked sense of humour (and who will rejoice if this book ends up in the bargain bin in

Woolies because no one buys it), the truly wickedest is Andy Gray. Andy is an incredibly funny man and has always had the capacity to reduce me to hysterical giggling both on and off the stage. He is bad and has no shame about trying to make you laugh in front of an audience. He took huge delight when he was watching an episode of *Superscot* and my picture appeared. There was a section in the programme that asked contestants to guess the identity of an actor or famous person from three photos of them as a baby, at school and present day. When my baby picture was put up the contestant buzzed and said "Jocky Wilson". Apparently Andy was running around his living room with joy and glee and enjoyed every moment of the slagging he gave me for the next couple of weeks. Apropos of nothing he would walk up and just say Jocky Wilson and we'd collapse. Thankfully the contestant got my identity from my school picture.

I did get my own back when a few weeks later Andy's pictures were on the same programme. At his baby picture someone buzzed and said "Robbie Coltrane", then couldn't recognise him from his school photo and worse didn't even recognise him when they put up his best spotlight still. Hey, that's showbiz!!!!!!!

Zola Budd and Jocky Wilson eh, what a talent.

*   *   *   *

After a hugely successful run at the Edinburgh Festival with *Naked Radio*, Colin decided that, rather than look for a new team of trendy young Oxbridge types at the Fringe, he would take a risk and do a TV comedy sketch show with the bunch he already had and supplement it with Helen Lederer and John Sparkes. That show became *Naked Video* which ran for six series and out of which came *City Lights* and finally *Rab C. Nesbitt*.

Of all the things I've done so far *Rab C.* has been the biggest hit with the public, and I'm always amazed at the warmth and affection people feel for Mary Nesbitt. But she deserves a chapter of her own, so we'll come back to her later. . . .

I have been really lucky to have been involved with these shows. I've also worked really hard, as women in this business have to. I have never just had the one job, I'm always doing something else like "opening Springburn", as Tony Roper would say!

12

THE NIPPY SWEETIES

Keeping up with this philosophy of never doing one job well when you can do four jobs badly, it only seemed natural that I'd be doing other things at the same time as *Naked Radio*. One of those things was the Nippy Sweeties.

Were we before our time or of our time? I am not quite sure, but the audiences loved it. The idea came from Liz Lochhead, as did the title. We had become very friendly during the show that she wrote for Wildcat and the TV play that I did. It was my first telly, and I think Liz's too, so there was a bond—apart from the fact that we were both from Newarthill and that I was in her wee sister Janice's class at school!

I loved Liz's writing and found her really funny and hugely encouraging, supportive and friendly. I was very much in awe of her and her abilities, and as usual covered it all by gabbing my head off and trying to seem confident. I am sure I drove Liz and Angie Rew, the other Nippy Sweetie, bananas. Here was this 25-year-old know-all telling these experienced writers and performers what to do, or voicing my ill-informed opinions. Sometimes I was right, but generally I was acting on instinct which I do a lot. I get hunches about things and I feel as if I know what would work and what wouldn't. I am a great one for reading about something, thinking it is wonderful and then wanting everyone else to agree with it. So this is a public apology to Liz and Angie if I was a pain in the arse.

Actually, I have always found working with women really enjoyable, especially when they are not forced into competing with each other. Generally, it has been joyful and liberating. The Nippy Sweeties was just that.

Liz got us together with a director, the lovely James Runcie, and we rehearsed in her living room in the West End. The material was sharp, funny and had something to say about a woman's place in 1985. We were feminists of the "Don't kick them too hard in the balls brigade" as one reviewer put it, but we kicked nonetheless and with a

Scottish accent. We were novel, I think, because of that. At the time there was a surfeit of women doing material about period cramps and Tampax. I tended to find them observant, angry, very hip but not all that funny. We were poignant and funny and if you were a man I don't think you felt that you had to wear a frock to get in.

We opened at Mayfest in Glasgow at the Third Eye Centre and it was sold out. This was due to Liz who was and is hugely popular. It was very scary but it went well. Next, we were asked to come and do a one-off gig at the Assembly Rooms in Edinburgh after our successful run in Glasgow and off we went. When we arrived, there were queues around the block and we assumed that something else must be on and then discovered the queues were for us!

We were pretty nervous by the time we got onstage, and during the opening scene I noticed that Liz was giving me completely weird cues and her dialogue was wandering. My only contribution to this section was to respond to Liz or back her up, but at one point she just stopped dead. I came out in the complete sweats and, seeing that Liz was in difficulty, ended up having a question and answer session with myself. I started saying things like "Well Liz, I know that you would say that blah, blah, but my answer would be blah blah and furthermore, I would venture blah, blah, and I know that you would say . . . ." The best laxative known to womankind. Sweat was pouring off us by the time Liz came back in with her lines. All of this probably took about two minutes, but it felt like an eternity to us. When we finally got off we collapsed in a heap and then Liz told us what had happened. The stage that we were on was built out of rostra and as Liz had started to speak she moved, the staging opened slightly and her stiletto heel went down in between and got stuck. She tried to pull it out and couldn't . . . and then of course you panic thinking that you are never going to get off the stage without leaving your shoe behind. You try to remain calm and work the shoe free but this is all going on while you are talking to an audience and before you know it you have no idea what you are talking about or where you are with the script! Scary stuff . . . poor Liz.

We were booked to return for the Festival, at the Crown Theatre. I am not a great fan of the Festival, and it has never really been that high on my list of things that I must do. It all seems very non-Scottish to me, and that is probably a good thing since we as a nation tend to gaze at our navels quite a lot, so it is good for us to gaze outwards a bit. When I lived in Edinburgh I loved how the City came alive, but didn't really rush to see hundreds of shows. All the schools were back (well not the public schools), so we were working and moaning about the traffic and not being able to get into the pubs. If we went to see something then it was usually something Scottish like a Wildcat show, or Borderline or Liz Lochhead. Much of that doesn't exist now in the Comedy Fest that is the Fringe and I think that is a shame because the people of Edinburgh like to be entertained too. In every show I have done there I have noticed that the audiences are ninety per cent Scottish in everything from *Naked Radio* to *Trumpets and Raspberries* or *Elaine With Attitude.* We had a very different audience from the trendy hip Londoncentric one which now exists. I think Liz crosses those boundaries, and the only time that I have ever been seen by the Perrier Award Judges was with Liz in the Nippy Sweeties. We were packed out and reviewed well, but we were women and Scottish so didn't make the short-list. I don't think women ever make it there.

Of course if you live in Glasgow you hardly know that the Festival is even on. You can be the hit of the Fringe and get a run at the Donmar in London and still die on your backside in Glasgow. Weird.

We may not have made the short-list but we were seen by STV, and they loved us—or so they said. There was a new regime there and they wanted to do something different—well not *Thingummyjig.* They wanted to lose that hand-knitted look and the new boys decided that we were it. We were very excited and thought that this was great, but soon found out that the people involved in the making of the programme hadn't a clue what we were about and set about trying to make us *Thingummyjig*. They took a very simple show with a piano and a wee bit of set with a writer/performer and two actress/singers and tried to turn us into a Variety show. We were caught between the devil and the deep blue sea.

All this cost them a fortune and the result was awful. They hired a seventies disco palace, got loads of cameras, gave us dance routines that had Liz in a complete state, having never had to do anything like that before. I had to go into a studio and record songs and then mime to them as we recorded the show and to top it all they shipped in fifty extras as an audience, who had to sit there all day and listen to all this being done over and over. We were knackered, exhausted, downhearted and depressed. Something that had started out so well had been ruined. They would have had a better show if they had just pointed the cameras at us at the live show in Edinburgh and cut it together.

But such is the nature of the great god television, which is full of people who have little or no knowledge of or respect for theatre and for what works. Being the bolshie git that I am, I decided to write to Gus MacDonald and complain and, to give him his due, he invited me up to his big corner office and listened to the grievances of a 25-

year-old actress and was extremely supportive. I later found out that Liz had done the same!

After that we all went off on our different paths, and I am glad to say that they continue to cross. But the TV thing probably killed us off as the Nippy Sweeties.

13

THE WEIGHT THING

When I meet folk in shops or in the street and they always feel free to comment on everything. I had a woman walk up to me in the street one day and utter those immortal words, "HO! are you that lassie aff that thing on the telly?" I swung round, smiled and said yes. She then poked me on the shoulder and said "well yer a loat wee'er" and that was it. Walked away. There was me thinking I'd at least get a "nice to meet you".

People comment on your size all the time. I can never get over what they notice. I was on a show on TV with the glam gear on and I got a letter from this woman commenting on my lovely brooch and asking if she could borrow it for a dinner dance that she was going to!

I was doing a show at the Cits years ago and Robbie Coltrane came to see it. We all went into the pub next door for a drink and of course up come the punters from the Gorbals to say hello to the Big Man. It's all "Heh, how you doin, Big Man, ye awright" and they're shaking his hand and slapping his shoulder, "naw man I was just saying to him, there's the man. Know, he's wan of us, a man of the people and he's funny, the lot." Robbie was being very polite and shaking hands and saying thanks and all that. Then the wee guy who's about four foot eleven and standing in awe of Robbie who's over 6 feet, shakes Robbie's hand and says. "Aye great, Big Man, great to see you, but you are a big fat bastard ain't ye?" Robbie was very gracious and said "Well I suppose you are right but I would've put it slightly differently myself." Now the guy didn't think that he was saying anything remotely out of order, he just felt that he had a right to tell Robbie what he thought.

Your friends tell you though don't they? And it is always the ones who have a problem with their own weight. The women that are naturally skinny (of which there are very few), who can't put on weight for love nor money, never ever notice whether you're any different.

My mum, for instance has had a weight problem and

she has been on a diet for 35 years and is of course now 2 stone heavier than when she started. But she is the first person to comment on other folk. She sees folk on the TV and says things like "Oh, hen I think you were badly advised to wear that the day, that does nothing for ye," or "That Anne Diamond has fairly put on the beef, Eh?" or "That Judy Finnegan is needing to get herself in hand, she's not looking good the now." This is coming from Ms World, of course. My mother is bad, but I have a friend whose mother told her the day after she gave birth to her third child "Now come on, you'll need to get rid of that stomach." Eh? It seems that for some women being fat is in the same category as murdering somebody, in fact worse in some cases.

I have a friend who is obsessed with her weight, dead controlled, asks for low-cal Perrier and calorie-free lettuce. She says things to me like "You look lovely darling and how is the weight?" Eh, just fine. I'm managing to keep a hold of my fat no problem, thanks for asking. Or "There's no doubt about it dear, fat is ageing." I know, if I hadn't been fat I wouldn't have a career, I've been playing 45 since I was 23! Always watch when a woman tells you that you look well—it means you look fat.

And before we go any further, television makes you look about ten pounds heavier than you are and about a foot taller. So in real life I look like a skinny munchkin.

As a woman on TV you've got all the same hang-ups as any other woman, but you do feel a bit more under the microscope when somebody points a camera at you.

Why is it that we feel this way? I mean men look in the mirror, stick out their spare tyre and say things like "Aye there's a lot of beer and money and hard work gone into that eh?" Or "I'll need to lose a few pounds, I'm getting a bit fat round the middle." Or "Eh, no bad for 40, eh?" Women look in the mirror and see that they are a bit overweight and they say "Oh God, I'm fat and ugly, untalented, boring, lazy, unlovable, I think I'll just kill myself." It's got to the stage that my husband can just look at me and say "Oh no, not another fat and ugly day" and then he hides for the next few hours, till I like myself a wee bit more. Madness.

Now I've read all the books about self-esteem and fat as a feminist issue, but they didn't make me feel any better, I still felt fat and ugly. And then you pick up a fashion mag and you see that none of the women in the photographs look like women, they look like girls or worse children, or more sinisterly they look like boys with wigs and stuck on silicone implants. What chance do we have? Where do we see the positive images of what women really look like?

But I gave in and decided after my last baby that something had to be done. You see having a baby is a great excuse. When they tell you that you can eat what you like if you breastfeed then I thought "that's for me". I took breastfeeding to mean eat as many bags of chips or Cadbury's Twirls as you can. Then you stop breastfeeding and comfort yourself by saying "I cannae get into those trousers, but I've just had a baby." I realised it was time to stop that excuse when Hannah hit 18 months!

The other excuse is that it is actually something physical that is making you fat, it is not that you eat too much. It's glandular, you have got this gland that makes you a greedy bastard.

You know things are bad when you go into the paper shop and pretend that you are buying sweets for the kids. "I'll have a Mars, a Twirl, two packets of crisps and what else was it they wanted . . ."

So, I thought, right. The slimming club. Admit defeat. And what a state I was in. Up to high do. You have nightmares that you'll walk in and the room will all turn round and point the finger and laugh. That they'll weigh you in front of everyone and shout out "14 stone—that's ridiculous" and everyone laughs. Or that you've got to stand up like in an AA meeting and say "Hello, my name is Elaine and I'm a fat bastard!"

But the reality was a lot easier. Like most things that women do we do them better when we don't feel so alone and we can support each other. There is a great feeling that you've all failed together and you can enjoy being fatties together. Unlike the aerobics class, where you feel like a failure as soon as you walk in because you're not wearing the right gear or you don't know all the routines. The first time you go to the class, you think that you look like the teacher, don't you? You think that all the movements that you're doing are the same as hers and you think that you must look like her as well. She, of course does 22 classes a week, works out in a gym and eats two bananas and a lean cuisine a day. I enjoyed the classes until I got a fright one day when I saw this pink blob in the mirror. Purple face, hair clapped to my head, not a pound hanging in the right way. But after a week on an iron lung I was brand new.

What is fascinating is not only the women who go to these classes, but the ones who run them. These women are born-again slimmers. Zealots—whose life is about getting everyone else to be thin and see the light. You know that they only keep their own weight down because they run these classes and they have to be thin—being thin is their life.

But what do we gain? We gain being acceptable. I feel normal. I can walk into a shop and pick up a size 12 and put it on and it fits. I can buy nice underwear instead of the Clydebuilt reinforced gusset variety. People compliment you on your weight and I think that they are really saying "Well, thank God you're not taking up as much room as you used to."

So how do I feel after all this struggle and self-denial? How do I really, really feel?

FUCKING STARVING!

14

THE TAIL AND THE DONKEY

During rehearsals for *Naked Video*, I was gabbing with Tony Roper. He is very funny, with a very wicked, black sense of humour, but he was always very kind to me when I first started out. If you want to find out someone's Achilles heel, ask Roper because he'll have it sussed. He is a great mixture of hope and optimism, coupled with suspicion and cynicism—like most actors actually. We're all pretty strange.

Anyway, during our chat he told me about a play that he had written called *The Steamie*. I said it sounded interesting and he asked me if I wanted to read it. Now this can be a bit of a Catch 22 situation. If someone you know and like shows you their precious work, and you don't like it, it can be a recipe for disaster. So I reluctantly said yes. Tony made me feel better when he told me not to worry if I didn't like it, because no one else did! Even though Borderline had commissioned it they didn't like it, and it had been turned down by every other company in Scotland. But Tony still thought it was good, so maybe I'd let him know what I thought.

As I went to bed that night I remembered that I had Tony's play to read. I sat in bed with a cup of tea, started to read, and I liked it. I thought it was funny and that it gave a really good picture of women's lives in the fifties. It had joy and pathos, and though sentimental at times, I felt that it could be improved by including some songs. I even marked the places where they could be added. I felt it would be perfect for Wildcat, as they had never done anything with such a strong female cast, and that a tour of Glasgow and Mayfest would be a big success.

I told Tony that I really liked it and that I would like to show it to Wildcat. They liked it and took it on. That was it. After all that time it just clicked. Years later, I asked the two Daves at Wildcat why they had gone with it and they said because I believed in it so strongly! Thank God it worked, I would hate to have been responsible if it had been a flop. Anyway, Dave Anderson and Dave Hicks set about writing songs and Tony and I got all excited about it. We talked about directors and asked David Hayman, but he was unavailable. Then Tony suggested the God-like creature that is Alex Norton. He was perfect. Apart from being funny almost all the time, with the filthiest sense of humour on the planet (which I love), he has great compassion and understanding. He directs with the knowledge of what it feels like to be an actor, and that is rare in a director. A perfectionist who rarely lets himself off the hook, he is also a bit of a bamstick with a tendency for histrionics if things are going badly. I had done his lovely panto at Borderline and witnessed his near suicide when we got it all wrong. Fortunately, Morag Fullarton was at the helm and calmed everything down, which she is great at—she has to be, considering the mental actors that she has had to work with!

When I first read *The Steamie* I cast it in my head. I saw Katy Murphy as Doreen, myself as Magrit (as did Alex, who thought I was too slow as an actress to play the wee, bustling Dolly), and I wasn't sure about the old woman, Mrs Culfeathers. But when I spoke to Tony he said, no, he wanted me to play Dolly. I couldn't understand that, as Dolly was sixty and I was twenty seven and I had always played busty Glasgow hardtickets like Magrit. But Tony insisted, and for some reason I went with it, as did Alex.

I was at most of the auditions and Katy was duly cast, as were Ida Schuster and Ray Jeffries. But Magrit was a problem, she was such an important part and the wrong person playing her can really affect the piece, as has happened in some subsequent productions.

Anyway, I was in Boots in Byres Road one day, when I heard this posh voice asking for "Slimachoc." I knew that voice, I knew that permanent slimmer. The one and only Dame Dorothy Paul. I think I pinched her bum and we ended up laughing and chatting and she asked me if I was involved in *The Steamie* and I said yes. She said that she would love to do it as she had done it at the reading of the play at the Tron. I told her that Magrit was not yet cast and that I would speak to Alex and Tony. I did so the next day and they thought it would be a good idea to see her. They did, and a "Tenement Goddess" was born (Dorothy visibly grew six inches when that review came out in *The Herald*!).

Rehearsals were not easy. It was all very new and we only had three weeks to get it on. We rehearsed at Wildcat's base in Jordanhill College and the show opened there. I still felt that I had made a big mistake in playing Dolly. Wandering around with bowly legs and my arse sticking out, I began to think that my career was about to nosedive into oblivion. Meanwhile Dorothy, who had not done a big play like this before and found learning such a huge part really hard, was very nervous, and the wonderful Ida was playing Mother Courage in a sink. We all felt worse because Katy was just perfect and had all her lines learnt by day three!

As we staggered towards the opening no-one knew what would happen. Although I had seen the potential in the show and had liked the play from the start, I still felt it lacked something—I was particularly worried that the mince section was far too long, and the imaginary phone call in the first act would never work. So what did I know! These turned out to be the play's two sure-fire set-pieces which, in footballing parlance, scored a goal every night for seven months.

The first night finally arrived, the theatre was packed and off we went. The stage was full of steam and, as it cleared, we could hear another show going on in the audience. The set was being discussed loudly and knowledgeably—"Aye Sadie that was the donkey where you hung your clothes to dry" (so called because it squeaked as it was pulled out and made an eeoh eeoh sound and because the technical term for it was a clothes horse). We soon discovered that the audience's reaction to the set was the same at every venue.

Despite the competition, we got started, but within ten minutes we could see that Katy was struggling and we soon realised that the smoke or steam was affecting her.

We got a signal to the stagecrew and somehow she got to the interval—during which she had a full blown asthma attack. But she still went on for the second act. What a trouper! By then we knew we had a hit. The audience loved it, and the theatre was filled with laughter throughout the performance. Although we had been rehearsing the play for three weeks, we were totally unprepared for the warmth of the audience's response. Our timing may have been all over the place, and the performance certainly wasn't perfect, but we knew that we had something special here.

The next day the tape in Wildcat's answering machine ran out due to the number of requests for tickets. Glasgow is like that. The reviews don't matter—word of mouth is what sells a show and if they like you, then you can run forever. We did.

Many things have been written about that play—not all of them positive. And certain productions have pandered to a couthy and cosy image that does not, in my opinion, do the play justice. But nothing will ever take the joy of that first tour away. It was magical. We didn't know what had hit us. I have never been in another show that got a standing ovation in Barlanark on a Saturday afternoon, had to stop in the King's Edinburgh because the audience got so hysterical that we couldn't get our lines out, and had, much to Giles Havergil's astonishment, the entire Citizens' Theatre on its feet. It also had the ability to reduce people to tears, when the women sang 'Roses are Shining in Picardy'. There ain't many pieces of theatre can do that. It was a huge chunk of my life, I did three tours of it, but nothing ever came near the first one.

There is nothing like touring in a hit knowing that every theatre will be full and that ninety-nine per cent of the time the folks will love it. Although Tony got a shock one night at the Cits, as he watched three people sit stony faced through the entire show. They never cracked a light as the rest of the audience were collapsing around them. When the curtain came down, Tony followed them out of the theatre—only to discover that they were Norwegian and obviously didn't understand a bloody word!

As a tour goes on, you get more blasé and confident and it's daft things that keep you amused—people saying the wrong lines or making silly mistakes. We love that sort of thing, because it's scary and it's not supposed to happen. But we almost came to a complete standstill as a cast one night in Kilmarnock.

On this particular evening, we were on good form and had a great audience. In the second act, I as Dolly was hidden under a sheet due to the fact that she had decided to take a bath in the sink. When, in the great comedy tradition, she is interrupted by the baths attendant, Andy, the girls cover her with a sheet to make it look like a pile of washing. As Dorothy was saying her lines I could hear her struggle and start to laugh. The more she tried to cover it up and carry on the worse she got. I whispered "What is it" as I couldn't see due to the sheet being over me. All I heard in reply was ". . . . stuck to his arse." I managed to peek out and saw that Ray had a pair of old tights stuck to the seat of his overalls but was totally unaware of his predicament. The more he moved around, the more they moved, and he kept looking at Dorothy as if she was on drugs or something because she and the audience just couldn't stop laughing. The more she tried, the worse she got. These old tights looked like a long tail and, even worse, Dorothy recognised them as being hers. Ray said that he left the stage thinking that Dorothy had taken a funny turn, but when he caught sight of himself in the mirror he collapsed laughing. We could hear him on the stage.

Apparently, he had sat on a cough sweetie that was on a chair, it had stuck to his bum and when he had come into our dressing room for a cup of tea he had sat on a chair with Dorothy's tights on it and inadvertently brought them onstage with him.

But these are the things that make us turns want to die laughing. A joyous moment.

By the time the telly version came around I was offered

the part but I thought I was far too young. The legendary director Hal Duncan did not think so, but I forced them to do a make-up test and I was proved right. I was twenty-nine and looked stupid trying to look sixty. I had also found out that I was pregnant and would have been eight months gone at the time of filming. Sixty and pregnant? I don't think so. I suggested Eileen Macallum as the person I would cast if it was my decision and I was right, she was great in the role.

I have to admit that it was hard to see it get all the accolades on telly. Not that I begrudged anyone their success, they deserved it, but it had been such a big part of my life for so long that it was hard to let it go. Such is the power of television that most people don't even know that I created the role of Dolly and I loved her so, but that's life. It happened in the theatre too. I was able to walk out of the stage door unrecognised, no problem, because people didn't think that it was that young woman who had played the part. It was a compliment and I used to have a quiet smile to myself as I walked past.

As luck would have it, if I had played the part on TV, I would have been unavailable for the pilot episode of *Rab C.* and I would have missed playing another woman that I love—Marydoll. So it was right, though it was sore.

But what a great time. . . .

15

THE WIT AND WISDOM OF AUNTIE MAUREEN

I've often thought about how I ended up playing all these characters on stage and television. For years now I've been so identified with a certain type of woman—the proverbial working-class hardticket. I just don't really know where it all started. I do know that I've always loved listening to women's conversations, particularly from this part of the world, and as a bit of a mimic I have observed and taken it all in for future reference. In my teens I realised that I had a talent for making people laugh, it was a way of getting out of trouble both at school and at home.

If you wanted to avoid being beaten up, be the class clown or daredevil and become known as "wee Smithie, she's a laugh!" Unfortunately, it got you great friendships with the boys but romantically it could put the kybosh on things if they saw you too much as a pal. I had to walk a very thin line.

At home it always got me round my mum and out of trouble. My mum has a great sense of humour and is a real giggler. In fact, it was her that brought Billy Connolly to our attention as she sat almost wetting herself and helpless listening to his sketch about the Crucifixion. I observed in my mum something common to women—that very determined desire to appear prim and proper only to blow your cool at the filthiest joke or risqué routine. I made her laugh either by imitating her, or my aunties or the neighbours, usually very cruelly, ending with her giggling and saying "Oh stop that, you're terrible" while reaching for the phone to tell folk what I had just said. I learnt the essence of timing here too, as there were times when she would go with it all and times when she would tell me that I was being far too cheeky. So I became very adept at working and sussing out my audience.

But the stuff that the women talked about among themselves fascinated me. They were very different when the men were there, only a few had the guts to be themselves when the men were around and some would even take them on, earning them a curious mixture of fear, derision and respect.

My Auntie Maureen was one of those brave women. She was very sharp and witty and above all fast. I'm sure that she had a wee book of put-downs and witty retorts for men under her mattress and studied it every night. There's a great story about her standing waiting for a bus. She had tons of shopping, it was pouring and she had been waiting for ages, but when one finally turned up it was full. She was furious and asked the driver if the next bus was going to be long. The driver, in true West of Scotland smartass style, replied, "I'd say it'd be the same length as this one" (Heh, heh with a grin you could happily have punched). Quick as a flash my Auntie Maureen says, "And will there be an effin monkey drivin that wan as well!" Off went the driver with his gas at a complete peep.

*   *   *   *

Even at parties I noticed that the men and women were different when they were apart. After a few quicksteps and a few more drinks the men tended to gather in the kitchen and basically talk shite. Well there's no other way to describe it is there? People that you know can't stand each other (like Uncles Peter and Frank) are hanging onto each other saying,

"Naw but ye don't understand, I love ye big man, I love you, I dae. Ye're great! I know I wind ye up aboot the Sellick and that, but it's just banter, ain't it? Ah mean it's never serious is it? Okay I shouldnae have lamped ye that time, but it's just that ah love ye (tears welling in eyes of both men) ah dae, yer a great guy. Billy what dae ah always say aboot Frank, he's great ain't he? Eh? Dae ah no say that? Am ah right or whit?"

Frank's reply is every bit as lucid. "Naw yer awright, ah'm awright. You're awright in't ye? Cos ah'm awright. Ho Bill, ah'm awright in't ah? See we're awright?"

At any time over the next two hours you could walk into the kitchen and this conversation would have progressed no further.

Having got rid of the men, the women were now able to get down to what they really wanted to talk about. The conversation moved very swiftly from ornaments to operations with great ease. But this could only be enjoyed with the men in another room. There was great competition between the aunts as well. Operation scars were war wounds and at any time you could enter the room to find their underskirts pulled up and scars and stitches being shown. Various phrases like "He was a bloody butcher that doctor, they ended up havin to gie me the 14 pints of blood. I was blue, Isa. Ye wid ah thought that ah had been painted wi a tin of blue emulsion."

No subject was more competitive than childbirth.

As soon as it was brought up, off they went. They didn't care that someone might be expecting or only fifteen like me and eavesdropping, they wanted to take the floor and give it laldy with all the pain and the drama.

Magrit: "You had a terrible time didn't ye, Isa? Oh aye. How long? Jeez, 22 hours, oh that's hellish! Me? Me? Ah wis four and a half weeks . . . but ah coped, ye know me!"

My Auntie Maureen always had the beezer of a story, though, and I think they all loved listening to her tell it because she was a great storyteller and because she always managed to top my nippy sweetie of an Auntie Magrit who could moan for Scotland. Maureen's stories had a sense of drama and she always managed to go up the gear shift too. She always started in first gear.

"Well as ye know lassies, ah had nae bother wi ma first two. They were oot in a jiffy, it wis just like shellin peas. But wi oor Alexander, it wis a bloody nightmare. It had been a long labour and he was a big boy—nearly 11 pounds (gasps from the women and a few grimaces), in fact I didnae walk right for six months! Anyway the afterbirth wouldnae come away and ah wis knackered. So ma doctor, lovely wee Asian doctor he was, he says to me, he says, 'Now don't you worry about anything, Maureen,' (she always seemed to be on first name terms with anyone she met. If she met the Queen she would be calling her Betty within five minutes!). He says 'ah've got the very thing for ye.' So off he goes. I'm lying there, desperate fur ma tea and toast and I turn roon tae find ma Alex (who has been bloody useless by the way!) draining a cup of tea and swallowing a crust. Ma bloody toast! If ah could've got oot that bed ah'd have swung for him, so I would.

"Anyway, ah'm lying there wi the legs in the stirrups when the wee doctor comes in with what I can only describe as a hubcap. He takes a run and fuckin jump onto ma belly. I screamed the place doon—but I have to tell ye lassies, it worked. That afterbirth wis oot in jigtime. Mind you there wis a helluva draft for aboot a fortnight but that wee doctor knew his stuff!"

The assembled women would all nod and ooh and ah at the appropriate moments but as a 15-year-old I was horrified! Years later when I found myself in a labour ward with the legs up in stirrups, I had all these visions from my adolescence. I'm sure the midwives were all bemused by my constant references to hubcaps and when they were going to arrive. It was the one area of relief in the birthing process that no hubcaps ever appeared!

Apart from that I have to admit that my Auntie Maureen was the only adult who ever told me the truth about childbirth. Something happens to women, when, expectant with your first child you ask the inevitable question "Is it sore?" An almost beatific look comes over their face and you can feel that something very patronising is about to be said, usually accompanied by some patting. "Ach don't you worry hen, you'll get through it." Conspiratorial looks are exchanged and smiles remain intact. When pushed my mother said "All I'll say is that it's the hardest day's work you'll ever do in your life." Well I would like to say here and now that I have had many a hard day at my work but I have never needed two epidurals to get me through it!

But Auntie Maureen took me aside and gave it to me straight. "Listen hen, don't listen to all this. It's bloody agony. It goes on for hours and hours, you think it's never gonie end, you can't eat or drink and you are stuck in some room with an eejit that tells you that if you breathe right it'll take the pain away. My arse!

"The eejit is usually, by the way, your husband who when he is not outside having a fly fag with the nurses then he's rubbing bits of you the wrong way and getting right on yer wick. My Alex fainted, and ended up with a bandage round his napper in all the photos. Don't believe any of that rubbish they tell you about the men. You are on your own, hen. All that stuff about men sharing the childbirth experience is shite. Mark my words hen, there will come a point during your labour when you will find yourself standing up in the stirrup screaming for morphine shouting this man is not my husband and by the way his parents were never married. A few days later you will have time to reflect on this, when you are sitting there on your rubber ring and you'll think, men sharing the childbirth experience? No way, Jose. Unless you've got a bowling ball stuck up your arse then you are not sharing the childbirth experience! So that's my advice hen plain and simple."

She was bloody right. . . .

16

MARYDOLL

From supermarket to pub to schools to walking around the streets, "Hello Marydoll" is a very familiar phrase to me. The vast majority of the time I cope with it and enjoy the fact that people identify me with a character that I love. It's great to know that something that you are involved in has such an impact. It would be great to think that at the start of *Rab C. Nesbitt* we all knew that, love him or loathe him, he and his friends and family were going to be such a success. But we didn't.

Many of us would like to think that we are a good judge of how things are going to turn out, but in this business "nobody knows nothin" as the old Hollywood saying goes. You can have the hottest writer in town, the biggest stars, the best director and crew and all have a whale of a time and yet, despite all that, the show will flop. You can have a writer who hasn't written anything decent in years, an alcoholic director, a cast who hate each other, a crew who go on strike every two days and it will be the biggest thing to hit the screen in ten years. Nobody knows.

When *Nesbitt* was first performed as a monologue in *Naked Video* in the 1980s, we thought it was funny. Gregor's performance was great and I personally loved the rage of this character who at that point didn't even have a name. Here was this guy who most people would cross the street to avoid, ranting and raving and howling at the moon (as we all have a tendency to do but usually in a more private location than Sauchiehall Street).

Yet the contrast between how he looked and what he said was hilarious. This was no Alf Garnett spouting half-baked, reactionary thoughts on the universe. No, these were well thought out philosophical musings induced by bad diet, smoking and alcohol and, although reactionary in some ways, it gave a voice to an underclass that had emerged in Britain during the 1980s. Ask the writer or anyone else involved if that is what we set out to do and they would answer, quite correctly in my view, "Actually, we just wanted to be funny."

The extreme reactions that people have to *Rab C.* are part of its success. I have met people over the years who adore it, know all the best lines, tape the shows and see all the live stuff. But I have also been pilloried by complete strangers, fellow feminists, and many po-faced socialists about the show's, in their opinion, patronising, jaundiced, insulting view of the working-class and the poverty of their lives. While I understand this view, and agree that certain boundaries are at times pushed to the limit of good taste, I do not think that these characters have no dignity or voice. Television cannot just be full of dramas and sitcoms about the daftness of the middle and upper-classes. The eccentricities and madness of the working-classes are every bit as amusing—though generally less pretty in the set department.

In an ideal world, it would be great if a situation comedy that deals with the hopelessness of people's lives could point towards the hope for a socialist society. But that would turn the show into a documentary, the humour would be lost, and the audience would disappear.

As a committed political animal myself, during the 1980s I found it almost impossible to watch films about abuse or poverty or unemployment or the decimation of the trade unions and our industrial base. Not because I didn't care or want to do something about it, but because they seemed to have little effect and apathy continued to grow. At the same time, disillusionment with government both local and national created a perfect audience for the humour and rantings of a class that the rest of society were desperate to ignore. And *Rab C.* was funny!

Even so, the snobbery that surrounds the programme is immense. Particularly amongst people in the media. They have swung from loving it, to wanting to kill it stone dead, to ignoring it, to loving it again. But they can't argue with the fact that an eighth series has been commissioned. People power is what counts—and the punters still watch it. There will always be nice middle-class people who worry that the English might get the wrong impression of us, and think that all television made in Glasgow should feature the Burrell Collection and various beautiful buildings, instead of shots of a derelict tenement and the black humour of a bandaged drunk. There are many answers to this, the first being that many people in England already have the wrong impression of us and nothing will change that. I also feel that we should grow up and stop looking at ourselves through the eyes of another nation and just get on with being what we are, and the Nesbitts of this world are surely a part of that.

No one tells Martin Scorcese that he shouldn't make *Mean Streets* or *Goodfellas* because they give a false impression of the levels of crime and violence in New York. People realise that there are many different facets to that great city and maybe we would do well to take note of that.

I've had people tell me that it is ruining my career (usually people who would jump at the chance of the part themselves), that I have become over-identified with it and how I will never be able to do anything else. It's true that I have encountered patronising attitudes and a limiting of job opportunities because of what has now become "Marydollism". I have found that disappointing and, at times, disheartening because it is not like being in a soap, where actors seem to be cast for the way they look and how close they may be to the actual written character. I am not deriding that in any way, simply saying that *Nesbitt* is different. All the main actors are exactly that—actors. We are not those characters, look nothing like them, and behave nothing like them. It is a tribute to the quality of the writing and the performances that people seem to believe that Rab, Mary, Jamesie and the rest really exist.

But out of all of this has grown a wee wumman called Mary Nesbitt and her wit, rage and confusion as she attempts to live some kind of a decent life are a joy to play. She ain't a pretty sight, and living next door to her would not be high on my fun-things-to-do list, but for some reason she is held in a great deal of affection by the public.

In conversations over the years with Ian Pattison, I have discovered that the character he originally wrote was very different from the one the public have come to know and love. In retrospect, I can see that he wrote her much harder and fiercer than I ended up playing her. When I first did a monologue as this woman with a black eye and fag, she was much harsher and darker.

I suppose I approached playing her against type. From an acting point of view, the easiest route to take is to go with one emotion allowing no light and shade, although this can mean the performance becomes one dimensional. To avoid this, you have to breathe life into a character and make them rounded. No one is harsh or vicious all the time. They laugh and cry and smile, however briefly.

When I started playing Mary, I thought of my Aunties and their initial hard edge, but I also remembered that forced cheeriness of the women from my family when things were at rock bottom.

This sounds like I sat and thought it all out in preparation for my part, dahling!!! But all this only became clear to me in retrospect. I am much more of an instinctive performer and tend to do things first and if they work, intellectualise later.

The first time I did a Mary monologue I had four days to rehearse it along with all the other sketches that week for *Naked Video* and was told after it that she was the wife of the guy with the bandage that Gregor had done in another monologue. It was to be another series later before the two characters got to meet. And it worked. The audience had taken Rab to their hearts and it was a joy to watch Gregor perform him. I did not know Gregor very well then, as I'd only done a couple of *Naked Radios* with him, so I was very nervous and very much in awe of this hugely talented and funny man. I craved his approval due to my own insecurities, but rarely got it. Although it made things difficult at the time, I am happy about that now because it toughened me up a lot and gave me more of an ability to hold my own. If you come into this game wanting other actors' approval all the time then you are on a hiding to nothing. Other actors are too busy with their own fears and insecurities to bother with anyone else's. If you said you could do it when you wrote in then your job is to get on with it.

So, seven series later, I still get a kick out of playing her and the reaction when I walked through the auditorium as Mary in *Elaine With Attitude* was wonderful, and at times overwhelming. When I decided to put *EWA* together I was unsure about putting Mary in, as I felt she might be seen as too hackneyed a device. So I put her in the second half after the interval, where she was more of a surprise and the audience had (hopefully!) already gone with the rest of the show.

Some of my friends said that they felt that I should have done more songs, but I had to point out to them that the vast majority of the audience were familiar with me only through television and thought I was fifty and seventeen stone. They certainly had no idea that I could sing! People who had seen me over the years in the theatre would know, but a few thousand people compared to four million is nothing. All the remarks about the TV show on Hogmanay and all the letters contained stuff about not knowing that I could sing or that I was so young. (At 40 that remark means so much!)

The purpose of *EWA* was to alter people's perceptions about me. There was a fixed view that I was the girl next door, from up a close in "Haw maw land", and I wanted to change that. I'm glad to say that the show served its purpose, but that does not mean that I want to reject Mary. I owe a huge debt to the creators of the series and enjoy playing her as much today as I did at the start.

Another common misconceptions is that because you are in a comedy then you must be having a laugh from the minute you start work to the minute you finish. That ain't the case. Yes, we do have great laughs, but the majority of the time you are trying to remember your lines, where to stand and to always hit your mark for the cameraman (the lovely John McNeil), to make sure that you walk to the right place for lighting, that you deliver your lines loud enough for sound (apologies to Mick Wild for the times I've been too loud and blown the wax out of his ears!), that the wig is looking as duff as the make-up girls (Julie and Heather) have intended it to, that the costume looks as close to the "Whit Evries" creation modelled by the citizens of certain schemes in Glasgow (with the naffest additions courtesy of Chez Holman, our designer) and finally that you don't break or eat the props (apologies to the beautiful George and Sammy, two of the nicest Huns and props guys in the biz, for eating the chips and for smashing the expensive fake Irn Bru bottle over Gregor's head when it was only a rehearsal and not a take—oops!!!).

Over the years the team have become like a family and although we have had many disagreements and can drive each other bananas, there is a great spirit the vast majority of the time. There has to be or it wouldn't be worth it. That is the thing that gets you up at 5.30am, into a wig and hacket costume, makes you stand on a freezing street in Balornock with weans and dugs running around in the rain, and some guy shouting abuse about licence fees.

Years ago, working on another show with Robbie Coltrane, we were filming in Scotstoun in front of a dilapidated close in a long row of tenements. When all the location vans with BBC written across the side arrived in the street they caused quite a stir. All the folk were coming down out of their flats to see what was going on.

Naturally there is always some smart arse who thinks he's big. As soon as they hear "ACTION" they open their windows and turn the stereo up. Great eh? When a request is made to turn it down, the reply usually ends with ". . . wankers". This duly happened and everyone was getting fed up when a wee wummin walked up and tugged the producer's arm and said "Excuse me, son, is this for those that havnie paid their licence?" The poor soul assumed that all these vans were detector vans out to get her.

The best location story I know is the (I'm sure apocryphal) one about the dog that kept barking every time the director said "ACTION". It was on some film shoot in Irvine or somewhere and the crew were getting fed up with this dog and the light was fading fast. But every time they yelled action, the dog would start barking. The crew asked who the dog belonged to and the weans said "That wummin up there, mister" and pointed to a window. The woman duly appeared at the window and when asked to quieten the dog she shouted "It's awright son, jist kick its baws and he'll stop barking." The production manager was horrified and just smiled and tried to get on with the shoot. But the dog kept on barking. He again tried to get the woman to do something but she repeated "Jist kick its baws son, he'll stop." As tempers frayed and the dog kept barking the p.m. gave up and booted this poor dog between the hind legs and it yelped and limped away. Only then did the woman say "Naw, his tennis baws son, they're lying in the grass!" Poor dog.

Anyway back to my point, it's the spirit and the team that keep us going, and of course the dosh!

When I look back at the seven series we've done, I have some great memories. The sight of Rab, Mary, Jamesie and Ella on bikes cycling around Rembrandtsplasse in Amsterdam gave me a real fit of the giggles. It was just so incongruous and the looks on the faces of the natives were wonderful. The sight of Rab in a kaftan *à la* 1970, Jamesie looking like a reject from *Department S* and *Jason King*, with the big lapels and sideburns, and Mary trying her best to look like Dusty Springfield had us all in hysterics.

The show also has great pathos at times. I found myself close to tears on set during the cancer episodes, when Mary had to walk down that corridor out of the ward thinking that Rab was dying. It was so well done and I could only think about that same journey that so many wee Glasgow women like Mary have made over the years, leaving the men that they have shared their lives with for better or worse, in a hospital ward dying.

The episode when Nesbitt's mother dies was also very moving. I found myself in tears watching it at home and had to phone Gregor to tell him that it was and is one of the finest pieces of acting I have ever seen.

But my favourite episode is the Spanish one that takes us to Fuengirola on a holiday that we have won. We had a great time there and the episode encapsulates all the comedy and pathos that this programme delivers at its best.

We had two weeks there and the worst thing was that it was filmed out of sequence, so we were not supposed to get a suntan or the shots wouldn't match. When you see the finished product, we have make-up on to cover up any tan. Bad news!

The whole episode is good from the start when they first win the holiday and then display all the classic expectations of sun and Spain. From the glee of arriving in their concrete hotel and Rab and Mary jumping on the beds with joy at their good fortune, to the beach scene with all four thinking that they are in a scene in *From Here to Eternity*.

My favourite line is actually something that Ella says to Jamesie. The scene is wonderfully set up, with great Pattison observations of working-class Northern Europeans and their bravado in the Mediterranean sun. It would only be natural that Jamesie in thong would refuse sunscreen on the beach saying that he didnae need it. Cut to four hours later and the lobster-like figure of Cotter is being stretchered off the beach into a waiting ambulance. As he leaves, Ella draws her long nails down his chest and leaves Jamesie screaming. When asked by Mary why she did it she replies "I wanted to gie him an idea of what a Caesarean feels like." Brilliant.

Another wonderful scene was when Nesbitt meets his mirror image, only the Spanish version. It was very moving. All of us had a lump in our throats, as Rab discovers his soulmate howling at the same moon in a different language. 'Twas ever thus.

I cherish many great memories of the national tour we did. There we all were with a huge chip on our shoulders thinking, in true Scots fashion, that English and Welsh audiences were going to hate us and that the show would die. The tour promoter, the wonderful Phil McIntyre, kept trying to tell us otherwise, but we were very wary. We did not know what was ahead.

We were doing one night stands up and down the country, and it was run like a rock 'n' roll tour. We were all from the theatre dahling and used to travelling in a minibus on tour, so when we saw our bus we were like kids. It was a genuine rock 'n' roll bus, complete with lounge area, video, cd, fridge, microwave—it was brilliant. We came to love it and hate it all at the same time, as we trundled up and down the M1 and M6 for four months, seeing parts of the country I didn't know existed. For the first time I understood why rock bands go mad and smash up hotel rooms. You are effectively trapped in a moving capsule with a group of people you work with. You cannot get off and you end up staying in one Holiday Inn after another until they all blend together. There are some towns on the tour that I know we played in that I can't remember anything about. It is a weird existence and can drive you a bit stir crazy.

Incidents stick out though, like being given our lunch free in a little cafe in Liverpool because the owners recognised Gregor and kept repeating "We luv the bones of you, we do. . . ." Gregor had asked me to go and help him find a jacket and I forgot just how recognisable he is. He was mobbed. I don't often get recognised until I open my mouth—due to the fact that I look a bit different without the wig on!

We got great reactions, standing ovations from Poole in Dorset through Reading to Newcastle and it was sold out everywhere.

Coming round the corner to the Hammersmith Odeon and seeing a sign saying *Rab C. Nesbitt* SOLD OUT was a great feeling. I had always dreamt of playing that theatre from my days in rock bands and imagined myself in funky gear strutting across the stage. But here I was in a bad blonde wig and orange tracksuit, unable to get my lines out for the roar of the crowd and it was magic.

The series has led to many great friendships, but the one with Babs Rafferty who plays Ella is very special. She is an extremely talented actress and a great friend. That means more than anything and is what sustains it all.

At this point it would seem completely ridiculous and heartless not to mention the loss and contribution of Eric Cullen to the series. People still pass comment on "wee Burney" and ask me for answers about what happened. I have none.

We got on well at work and enjoyed a good laugh together. We became close, as work mates do over a period of years, and I knew that abuse was a huge scar from his past, but like many survivors of incest he gave the impression of someone who was coping and who had dealt with it.

Outwardly he was funny, kind and good company. He was mischievous and was good at sending himself up as he did once when he suggested on the tour bus that he should be put up on the luggage rack so he could get a decent sleep. Much drink had been taken so we all thought that it would be great to try and get him up there—naturally we failed and he ended up on his backside on the floor in a heap with the rest of us.

Eric was a curious mixture of intelligence, fragility, insecurity and a massive ego. He had a huge heart. He was a terrible upstager and would do almost anything to pull the focus away from other actors back to him. Why he felt he had to is anyone's guess, as he was 4' 4" tall and everyone was watching him automatically! He and I had a few run-ins over his upstaging and his personal addiction to laughter—any laughter as long as it was for him, but he would take it on the chin, have a laugh and go out and do the same the next night!

I was working in St. Andrews when the news of his arrest broke. I was horrified and managed to find Eric and speak to him. He was devastated and my only advice was that he should get out of the country until the truth could be established. It was awful. Unfortunately, he took the advice of some media person and the next thing I knew there were front page confessions and a feeding frenzy had broken out between the tabloids. To this day I do not know the truth.

I would like to say at this point that I was a good friend to Eric through all his pain but I wasn't. I did write and phone but as Eric withdrew from everyone we were all left not knowing what to do and it all drifted.

His death was a shock and naturally very upsetting. More importantly it was a great tragedy for his family and those he loved. I was very upset but made a decision by myself that I did not want to go to the funeral when I read that "hordes of showbiz celebs were expected to attend". I thought, no, I am not going to participate in some sort of circus. The papers wanted a photo of the Nesbitts in mourning and I felt that would be so awful, when Eric's real parents who had already suffered so much as the good people they are, were the people who needed help and support. They had been through enough and I would have felt like a hypocrite since I hadn't seen him for so long.

When I think of Eric I remember his kindness, his mischievousness and all the laughs we had.

17

A VIEW FROM THE FRIDGE

One of the recurring spiritual themes in my life is chocolate, ever since those days at the Wee Free Sunday School when we got our bar of chocolate as a reward for enduring the service. I have seen chocolate as a reward ever since—it hasn't rewarded my hips very much but my soul has felt better. I feel that I should pay homage to it for all the blood sugar it has boosted since the moment I first sat down at this word processor all those months, nay, years ago.

Chocolate helped me write my show, sustain me through the rehearsals, then the arduous touring and performing of the show, too. What a drug!

My fridge is full of fun-size chocolate (well they are always fun for me) and the fridge is also a recurrent theme because it's got all the sweeties in it. I have eaten hunners as I sit at this bloody word processor, only stopping for a game of my other passion—tennis. Yes, very middle-class. Not many tennis champs from Cranhill are there? But I love it. Finally, after a lifetime of forcing myself to do a sport, I have found one that I adore and can play. I'll never make Wimbledon, but I can play. It is the only thing that I do that allows me to switch off and not think about work. I know that I have driven the girls in the club bats with this book, and finishing it will be as much of a relief to my doubles partner Christine as me, because she has had to endure each chapter with me, when all she wants is for me to hit the ball back over the net!

I have also stopped occasionally to speak to my children who have had to endure a very preoccupied and crabbit mother. One day they will understand or they'll have a lot of therapy. I can see it all now. The lurid headlines *à la Mommie Dearest* and I will be cast as Joan Crawford. To everyone else she was poor old Marydoll, to us she was the mother from hell. Read "Mary Dearest" and find out the truth!!!

When you start dredging up who you are and where you came from it does have quite an effect on you and I have found it hard and enjoyable all at once. My favourite subject at school was history and I always thought that those stories of kings and queens and wars were what was important. But what is really important are the stories of ordinary lives and the twists and turns they take on their journey. That is as valid an account of history as any life of a monarch. It gives a flavour of life at the time that a dry set of dates cannot. *Angela's Ashes* said more about the poverty in rural Ireland in the early part of this century than any textbook I ever read.

At this point in the story so far, I am supposed to become deeply philosophical and impart some of the great wisdom that I have acquired on my journey. Well I am sorry but I can't—which will no doubt be a relief to you in that I have not devised some sort of homespun, morning television, quick fix on life.

So here I am looking from my fridge full of chocolate and surveying the surrounding landscape. Generally, I suppose I would have to say that, compared to some people's lives I have had it pretty good. By that I don't mean that it has been a cakewalk but I do have to count my blessings. None of us are very good at appreciating what we really have in life and what I do know is that blessings have nothing to do with fame and fortune. They are to do with very simple things in life, mainly love, of one's family, friends and partner. I wish I could live my life every day remembering those facts, as I rush headlong into another needless bout of insecurity and avarice.

It has been a pretty good journey so far. I have gone further than any map I was equipped with could show me and I feel lucky. Lucky that I had the family I had, lucky that I was alive at a time when an education was seen as a right not a privilege.

I feel lucky to be in showbusiness at a time when not having a public school accent was not a drawback. There is a lot of talk about the dumbing down of the arts and media, and while I would agree that I find much of the lad and ladette youth culture totally boring now (and I want to punch Chris Evans and Danny Baker more and more frequently), I do see this as a positive step compared to the patronising, boring public school closed shop of the past. The masses are seeing themselves reflected for the first time and though it may not be pretty or challenging, it is a proper swing of the pendulum towards a balance in the Arts that ends the type of class-ridden racist snobbery that prevailed for so long.

I feel lucky that I was around when having a view on the political situation was seen as a good and natural thing. I was brought up to believe that speaking out about injustice and what was and is unfair in life was right and that if lots of people felt the same way then we could change things for the better. It is now seen as a bit wet and a waste of time and much as I do understand and share some of the apathy and disillusionment with the boring suits that govern us, I am too much of an optimist and old hippy to become one of the hedonistic bunch of blonde bimbettes that grace our screens telling us what we should be.

I feel very lucky that I was around in a generation that told men that women were not their property and that beating them up for not cooking the tea right was, is and always will be totally wrong. That women had a right to be married or single, that they could have a career and children (though it is bloody knackering) and that men were allowed to share in child-rearing and get to know their children without being thought of as poofs!

I feel lucky that I was allowed to be part of the process for Devolution for Scotland and hopefully I'll still be rabble rousing during our first Parliament and beyond—maybe we'll even get to manage our own finances in time, but I fear that may only come with independence. No I am not standing for Parliament this time. I would very much like to at some point in the future but my work commitments are such that it would be impossible. I think that the Tories and others have enough ammunition on me without allowing them any more gags about Marydoll on the front benches. It is a bad gag I grant you, but politicians are rarely witty or clever so it is to be expected. Personally I think that a few more of the Marydolls of this world in Parliament would be wonderful and probably help give a voice to those who have been ignored for too long.

So I am lucky so far but who knows what lies ahead. If you had told me two years ago that I would write a book then I'd have laughed. Yet, here I am writing—me, writing . . . who'd have thought . . . writing and eating chocolate . . . from the fridge. Of course the fridge door opening has always had a special significance for me too. As that light went on I was performing and showing off like someone with too much extrovert energy, as my maths teacher so rightly pointed out all those years ago. All my life I have been a performer, an over-achiever. When that fridge door opened and that light came on, off I went whether anyone wanted me to or not. Life is simpler now in that now I just go into the fridge to steal my children's chocolate!!! The weird thing is that I have married a man who hates sweets. Something very Freudian there no doubt.

Fortunately I married a man with taste and class (obviously an off-day when he picked me—but we did meet at a Union meeting, so he was probably all fired up about a demo or something and I got in the way!!) He is good for me because he is not impressed by desperate performing or attention-seeking behaviour, so the older I get the more I am able to accept that tap dancing won't make people like you if they don't. It is about your own approval and those honest, truthful friends who have been there through thick and thin. That is all that matters.

I was 40 a few weeks ago and it does feel different. I have a sense of precious time running out that has nothing to do with fame or fortune. It is about seeing my children's faces every day, loving my husband and treating him right, caring for my friends and family. It all becomes quite simple.

Having survived a lot of the angst in my life, I now cherish a wonderful mother, a great dad, two kind thoughtful caring sisters who have dealt with the vagaries of having a famous sister and done a lot of babysitting too. I have a great, strong and loving husband and two daughters that I could not ever have imagined loving so much.

I have had great luck and good fortune and that has helped carry me through on the limited talents that I have been given. I am not being falsely modest when I say that. I am grown-up enough to look objectively and to see that I have some talent. I am an alright actor, an alright singer, but I do tell a good story. (Sorry I went all Lanarkshire there and wanted to erase that for daring to praise myself and possibly overstep my "Moira".) No , I am going to be bold and say that I can do something well, and I communicate well. I don't care if the Gods strike me down for it. I think that the skill of communicating comes from my Irish side and my grandfather who was wonderful at communicating and entertaining strangers but not so good with his kin! Classic actor psyche there, but that is another book!

My friend Dave Anderson once introduced me at a benefit concert as one of the best communicators he had ever met. I was actually a bit disappointed as I hoped that he was going to introduce me as one of the best actors or singers he had ever met. Now I know what he meant and I thank him. If you have got to the end of this book then I must be communicating something, eh?

I had a big party for my 40th and I was surrounded by a couple of hundred friends and family. The aunties all turned up and Auntie Maureen was there in pink and up for anything. She seems to still like me and thinks I am doing alright. That's enough for me. She told me a long time ago to hitch my wagon to a star and I suppose I did. The star was made up of people like her. I don't want to get all soppy and religious but I will for a minute. I feel quite blessed and I don't really know why I have been given all this love and luck. I suppose my duty is just to appreciate it, enjoy it and put something back. As we stand close to a Parliament for Scotland and a new millennium, I hope I get the chance to do just that. . . .